Harry de Windt

The New Siberia

Harry de Windt

The New Siberia

ISBN/EAN: 9783744717502

Printed in Europe, USA, Canada, Australia, Japan

Cover: Foto ©ninafisch / pixelio.de

More available books at **www.hansebooks.com**

THE NEW SIBERIA

BEING AN ACCOUNT OF

A Visit to the Penal Island of Sakhalin, and Political Prison and Mines of the Trans-Baikal District, Eastern Siberia

With Appendices, Map, and Twenty-Eight Illustrations

BY

HARRY DE WINDT, F.R.G.S.

AUTHOR OF
"FROM PEKIN TO CALAIS BY LAND," "A RIDE TO INDIA," "SIBERIA AS IT IS,"
ETC.

LONDON: CHAPMAN AND HALL, Ld.
1896

To my Sister

PREFACE.

I HAVE endeavoured, in the following account of my latest Siberian experiences, to avoid, as far as possible, any reference to Government statistics. The latter would only weary the general reader, and perhaps lead to controversies which, experience has taught me, conduce to very little more than the waste of good ink, pens, and paper. Questions of special interest connected with the Russian Exile System will be found in the Appendices.

The probability of the total abolition of exile to Siberia in favour of deportation by sea to the Island of Sakhalin has suggested the title of this work, which contains little more than a series of sketches illustrative of life and travel in the remoter parts of Asiatic Russia. I may add that in no other case has permission been granted to an Englishman (or other foreigner) to travel on, and have the free run of, a Russian convict ship, to visit the prisons in the interior of the Island of Sakhalin, or to freely associate with political exiles actually undergoing imprisonment at the mines of Nertchinsk.

HARRY DE WINDT.

San Francisco, *27th March*, 1896.

CONTENTS.

CHAPTER I.
NAGASAKI . . . . PAGE 1

CHAPTER II.
THE PRISON-SHIP 9

CHAPTER III.
"OLGA" 31

CHAPTER IV.
THE ISLAND OF SAKHALIN (KORSAKOVSKY-POST) . . 50

CHAPTER V.
THE ISLAND OF SAKHALIN (ALEXANDROVSKY-POST) . . 81

CHAPTER VI.
A JOURNEY IN THE INTERIOR. (IN TWO PARTS) . . 111

CHAPTER VII.
VLADIVOSTOK AND THE SIBERIAN RAILWAY . . . 138

CHAPTER VIII.

ON THE ROAD 167

CHAPTER IX.

THE OUSSOURI AND AMOUR RIVERS. BOUSSÈ—KHABAROVSK 188

CHAPTER X.

THE UPPER AMOUR AND SHILKA RIVERS. KHABAROVSK—
STRETYNSK 202

CHAPTER XI.

THE SILVER MINES OF NERTCHINSK. (IN TWO PARTS) . 233

CHAPTER XII.

THE LOWER AMOUR. KHABAROVSK—NIKOLAEFSK . . 283

APPENDICES AND MAP.

LIST OF ILLUSTRATIONS.

PORTRAIT OF AUTHOR	*Frontispiece*
	PAGE
ARRIVAL OF CONVICTS, ODESSA RAILWAY STATION	11
GROUP OF CONVICTS ON THE "YAROSLAV"	13
GROUP OF CONVICTS BOUND FOR SAKHALIN	17
A RUNAWAY CONVICT, ISLE OF SAKHALIN	21
CONVICT TYPES	23, 25, 27
DOG POST—SAKHALIN TO EUROPE. "ON THE ROAD"	51
GOING TO WORK. ALEXANDROVSKY-POST	87
ALEXANDROVSKY-POST, SHOWING, ON THE RIGHT, MR. TASKINE'S HOUSE	89
THE "PLET" AND MANACLES AS NOW USED ON SAKHALIN	93
FIXING FETTERS, ALEXANDROVSKY-POST, SAKHALIN	95
CONVICT CHAINED TO WHEELBARROW	99

LIST OF ILLUSTRATIONS.

	PAGE
GROUP OF CONVICTS, ALEXANDROVSKY-POST	107
BEARDED AINU AND GILYAKS, SAKHALIN	115
ROAD-MAKING—THE DINNER HOUR. SAKHALIN	125
SOPHIE BLOEFFSTEIN, "THE GOLDEN HAND"	131
THE "GOLDEN HAND" AFTER HER FIRST ESCAPE AND RE-CAPTURE. SAKHALIN	133
NEAR NOVA-SILYA, TRANS-SIBERIAN RAILWAY	169
PANORAMA OF KHABAROVSK	205
GOVERNOR'S HOUSE, BARRACKS, AND PART OF OLD PRISON, AKATUI	255
THE GOVERNOR AND PRISON WARDERS, AKATUI PRISON	259
COLONEL ARCHANGELSKI	277
GILYAKS, SAKHALIN	289
MAIN STREET OF NIKOLAEFSK	297
PLAN OF "KAMERAS" ON S.S. "YAROSLAV"	305
PLAN OF PRISON OF ALEXANDROVSKY-POST, SAKHALIN	307

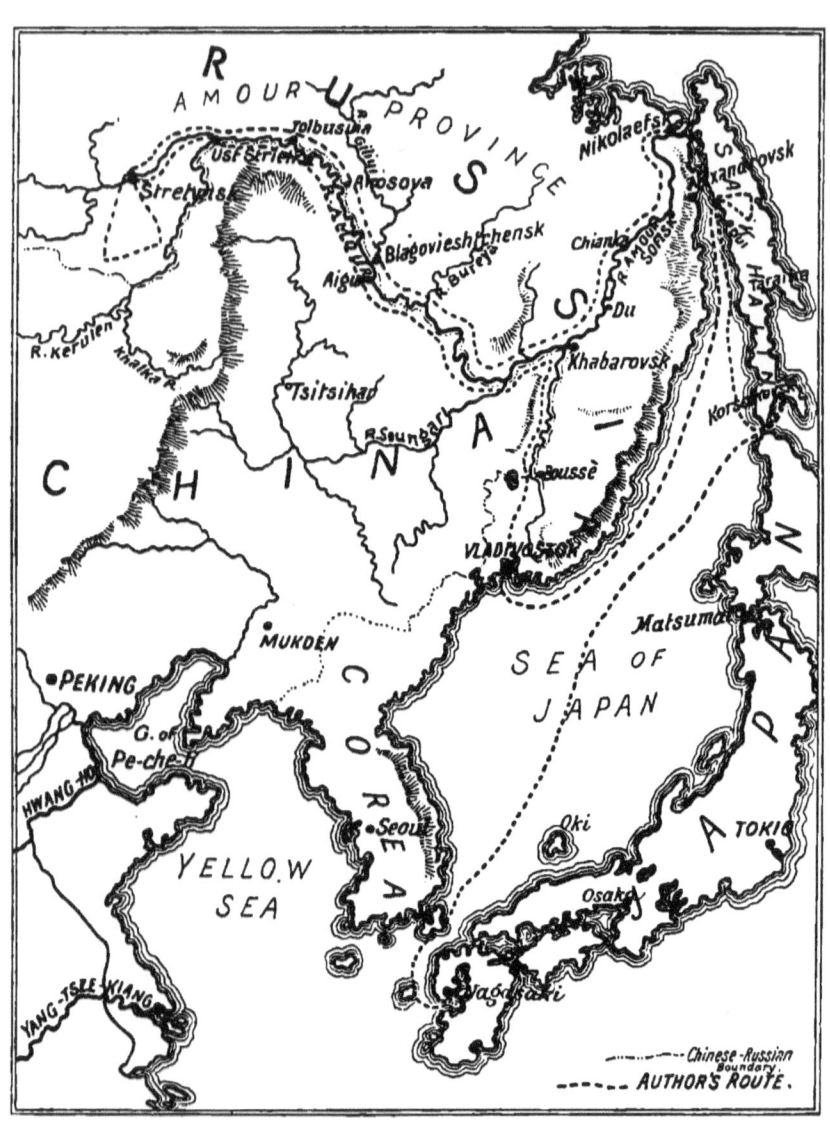

THE NEW SIBERIA.

CHAPTER I.

NAGASAKI.

IT is early spring-time in Japan, in the year 1894. The fragrant blossom-scent is in the air, and peach and almond petals litter the narrow streets, and dab snowy patches on the dark hill-sides around Nagasaki. As the *Yaroslav* slowly steams through the blue, lake-like harbour towards the open sea, I watch the sunny toy landscape fade with regret. My days in the land of laughter and "Jinrikshas" have flown all too quickly, and I have to-day said farewell to pleasant travelling companions. Now I feel lonely enough, which is scarcely surprising, for I know not a soul on board, to say nothing of the fact that the *Yaroslav* is a Russian convict ship.

She was not a beauty to look at. It was not without serious misgivings that I climbed up her rickety gangway ladder that bright April morning, and stood at last upon her grimy deck. The contrast, after a trim P. and O. steamer, was more striking than pleasant. I looked, with some surprise, in vain for signs of this prison-ship's human cargo. She seemed, although on the point of sailing, almost deserted. Half-a-dozen high-booted, slovenly-looking Cossacks in rusty green uniforms lounged listlessly on their rifles, basking in the sunshine, about the gangways. The captain and his gold-laced, white-capped officers were consuming tea and cigarettes under an awning aft, but not a solitary convict was visible. It was only when, awaiting admittance, I had become somewhat accustomed to the novel surroundings, that I was able to distinguish a dull murmuring sound like the distant roar of the sea. I then realised that the convicts were now (the invariable rule in port) securely confined in the "Kameras" (public cells) between decks, but that silence is not enforced was evident by the occasional bursts of laughter and song that arose from below.

"You cannot go," was the captain's curt reply to my request. "We do not carry passengers."

But my never-failing permit from St. Petersburg soon righted matters, and I experienced that same evening the strange and not altogether agreeable sensation of being out on the open sea, "cabined, cribbed, confined," with nearly eight hundred of the most dangerous and desperate criminals in European Russia.

Cabin accommodation on the *Yaroslav* was extremely limited, for the prison-ships of the Russian volunteer fleet do not as a general rule carry passengers. I shared a tiny malodorous den with a military bandmaster from Odessa, a quiet, inoffensive little man of Polish extraction, and dubious, not to say unclean habits. The "Kapellmeister's" society would have been bearable but for his violin practice, which often extended far into the night, to be resumed at daybreak. But he was a cheerful, good-tempered little soul, which atoned for much, though not perhaps for his nocturnal efforts on the clarionet, on which instrument he was a beginner.

We were out of sight of land by six o'clock that evening. An hour later, the inevitable "Zakouski" in the pretty ward-room had preceded an excellent dinner, at which Captain Ostolopoff and his officers, five in number, were present. The refinement and luxury of the apartment in which we assembled was a striking contrast to the rest of the ship. One's feet sank in soft, glossy Bokhara carpets, fine proof engravings covered the walls of white enamel picked out with gold, and a cottage piano stood in a corner, while low Turkish divans surrounded three sides of the room, the fourth being partly occupied by a broad stairway leading to the upper deck. The ward-room of the *Yaroslav* was suggestive of anything but a convict ship.

The "pope" or priest, the doctor, the little Kapellmeister (in full uniform), and myself, completed our party at dinner, with one solitary and striking exception. This was a pretty, dark-eyed girl of about eighteen, who seemed shy and nervous, and strangely out of place amid this masculine element. It was not until some days had elapsed that I learned her strange, pathetic story. Russians are as reticent about such matters as they are ever hospitable and ready to welcome a stranger in their midst. I could not have received a more cordial welcome from my own countrymen on board a British warship, than that given me by these Russian officers, who were for the most part drafted from the Imperial navy; one, indeed (Lieutenant Borkovski), from the Imperial yacht *Livadia*. My first meal on board the *Yaroslav* was a pleasant surprise. Seated at a table covered with snowy linen, and sparkling with glass and silver, discussing a *cuisine* that would not have disgraced a first-class Parisian restaurant, one could scarcely realise that only a few feet below us were collected close upon a thousand of the vilest criminals in Europe—the very sweepings of the slums of St. Petersburg, Moscow, and Odessa.

Although acquainted with the Russian language, I was glad to find that every one (with the exception of the priest) spoke French, and Lieutenant Borkovski, who had superintended the building of the *Yaroslav* in Scotland, a few words of English. Borkovski was enthusiastic in his praises of London, but he did not think much of Glasgow on a Sunday. The Salvation Army especially excited his ire, and he marvelled how a civilised people like the English could tolerate a foolish fanatic like "Mr. Boots."*

Night had fallen when, after cigarettes and coffee, I took leave of my pleasant hosts, shaking hands with each in turn, as is the fashion after every meal in Siberia. The sky was ablaze with stars as I left the ward-room to smoke a final cigar, for discordant and ominous wheezings from the direction of my sleeping place warned me that rest, for the

---

* General Booth.

present at least, was out of the question. Save for a silent and motionless sentry here and there, the decks were deserted; but the night was close, and, for coolness' sake, the fore and aft hatchways had been thrown open. Looking down into these from the upper deck I could discern, in the bright electric light, some twenty or thirty linen-clad figures sitting or lying about the square iron grating surrounding the hatchway. Some were chatting, others reading, and all seemed orderly and well-behaved. Some, especially the younger men, had a tired, pallid look on their faces that told of weary days and restless nights in the stifling heat of the tropics, and most of those that I subsequently saw had been more or less affected by the long and trying sea voyage from Odessa.

As the ship's bell struck the hour of nine there was a sudden movement in the group. All rose to their feet, and immediately after, the priest, preceded by a sailor bearing a lantern, passed me slowly, descended to the main deck, and took up a position immediately over the hatchway. For a few moments his voice fell softly on the still evening air. There was a pause for a few seconds, and then, with a wild wave of melody, followed the beautiful evening hymn, which, although familiar to me, had never seemed so impressive as out upon that lonely sea, amid those grim surroundings. A few minutes more and the service concluded, the guard was set for the night, and silence again reigned, broken only by the swirl of the sea and rhythmical beat of our screw. The human cargo of the *Yaroslav* was safely battened down until another dawn should bring them a stage nearer to their dreaded haven—the Island of Sakhalin.

CHAPTER II.

THE PRISON-SHIP.

THE *Yaroslav*,* a twin-screw steamer of over 3,000 tons register, was built expressly for the Russian transportation service by Messrs. Denny, of Dumbarton, in 1892. She belongs to the " Dobrovoilno Flott," or " Volunteer Fleet," which was formed shortly after the Russo-Turkish war by private enterprise. The fleet is, however, largely subsidised by Government, and in the event of war its ships would be utilised as armed cruisers.

The transportation season commences in April, and ends in October, when the navigation north of Vladivostok is closed by ice. Convicts for Sakhalin are brought by rail from

* See Appendix A.

various parts of Russia and embarked at Odessa, whence they proceed to their destination *viâ* Suez, Colombo, Singapore, Nagasaki, and Vladivostok, the eastern terminus of the Trans-Siberian Railway. While on board, the convicts are in charge of the first lieutenant, who is furnished with the "dossier" of every man. This document, which on arrival is handed to the Sakhalin authorities, bears the full name, description, and photograph of the convict, also a list of the articles supplied to him on embarkation. This custom has, to a large extent, done away with the practice of exchange of name and sentence, at one time so common in Siberian prisons. The *Yaroslav* carried no female convicts, the latter being kept rigorously apart, and despatched in special ships.

"Light a cigarette," said Ivanoff, the first lieutenant, after breakfast the next morning, "and I will take you around the 'Kameras.'"

Civility forbade my refusing, although I should have preferred to visit the holds out of reach of official surveillance. Such a proceeding would, I felt, detract considerably from the value of my investigations. But the lieutenant soon reassured me by adding:

"I will show you the run of the ship, and

ARRIVAL OF CONVICTS, ODESSA RAILWAY STATION.

you can afterwards inspect her alone, and at your leisure."

This I eventually did, visiting the wards unattended, two or three times a day (and once by night), and conversing freely with the convicts.

I follow my guide through a group of

prisoners at exercise on the foredeck, and here he pauses for a moment to receive the report from the chief warden for the day.

"They are allowed on deck every day in fine weather, in batches of twenty," says Ivanoff, disappearing down the companion ladder — whither, grasping the brass hand-rail, I follow him. Diving out of the dazzling sunlight into the dimly lit fore-hold, some moments elapse ere I can distinguish my surroundings; but gradually becoming accustomed to the gloom, my eyes presently light upon a strange scene indeed. There is nothing tragic or repulsive about it. I remember that my first impression was one of wonder that so many human beings could be packed into so small a space, and yet suffer, apparently, so little inconvenience. Ivanoff's appearance was the signal for a deafening shout of "Good day" that fairly shook the deck above us. "Good morning, brothers," was the lieutenant's response, as he beckoned me to follow him closely, two soldiers with loaded revolvers accompanying us.

GROUP OF CONVICTS ON THE "YAROSLAV."

On the occasion of my voyage the *Yaroslav* carried 797 male convicts, which, as she is constructed to accommodate 802, was about her complement. The ship is divided into four large "Kameras," or public wards, two forward, and two abaft of, the engines. These contained respectively 184, 172, 240, and 201 men. These "Kameras" are each ventilated by an enormous hatchway, and four large portholes on either side of the ship, which are invariably kept open night and day. In heavy weather, however, it sometimes becomes necessary to batten down, and air is then supplied by means of electric fans. Notwithstanding all these advantages, I am told that the sight of one of these convict-holds during a typhoon (and the latter occur chiefly in the transportation season) baffles description. The intolerable suspense, the howling of the tempest, the stifling heat, and worst of all, the darkness (for the electric light is often extinguished), transform the usually quiet and well-ordered "Kameras" into veritable "Infernos." I have gone through the same terrible experience on board one of the floating hotels of the Canadian Pacific Railway Company, and judging from my own sensations on that occasion, when surrounded by light, luxury, and cheerful companionship, can readily conceive the sufferings of poor wretches penned up like rats in a cage, dreading the end with every sea that crashes overhead, and, in the event of disaster, almost inevitably doomed to destruction. But typhoons are fortunately not of very frequent occurrence, and the Russian prison-ships have up till now been singularly fortunate in this respect. There is no doubt that, apart from climatic conditions, which in the Red Sea and Indian Ocean are necessarily severe, the Sakhalin convict is far better off than his prototype on land, for the march across Siberia is, even under the most favourable conditions, infinitely more trying than the journey by sea.

A further examination of the holds showed that they are eight feet in height, the oblong spaces under the hatchways being kept clear by means of iron gratings. These gratings, which subdivide the four principal "Kameras" into smaller compartments, also completely surround them, forming a corridor three feet wide

GROUP OF CONVICTS BOUND FOR SAKHALIN.

between the bars and bulkheads—a very necessary precaution. This circumstance has more than once given rise to the absurd report that Russian convicts are kept in cages on board ship! The "nares," or wooden sleeping platforms, are arranged on the same system as those of the Siberian prisons, and, although there are no separate bunks, a space of six feet by three feet is allotted to each man. Many of the convicts had pillows and some mattresses, although neither of these are provided by the Government. I remained nearly a month on board the *Yaroslav*, and during that time scarcely a day passed that I did not visit the holds; but I never found the latter anything but scrupulously clean and absolutely free from smell, for in addition to the ventilation from hatchways and portholes, the lavatories are kept sweet by a constant current of fresh air pumped through them by the engines. It is not surprising that, amid these surroundings, the prisoners themselves appear far better cared for than those I had seen in Siberian "etapes," where the difficulties and hardships of outdoor travel through wild and lonely regions, render cleanliness a very secondary consideration to the convict, tired out by a long tramp through mud, wind, and rain. The clothing supplied to the *Yaroslav* exiles was good, and well adapted to the climate of Sakhalin, though rather thick for the tropics; but this difficulty is generally overcome by discarding the gray cloth trousers and overcoat that are worn over the linen shirt and drawers. I can vouch for the quantity of the food.* It is amply sufficient, and an idea of its quality may be gleaned from the fact that on a "shtchi" (cabbage broth) day, soup from the prison coppers was served at the officers' mess—and uncommonly good it was. I was surprised to find that not only smoking is permitted during exercise hours on deck, but that one pound of tobacco is presented to each man on embarkation at Odessa. It is coarse, rank stuff, but convicts are not fastidious regarding the fragrant weed, as Portland and Dartmoor can testify.

There are, in all, four punishment cells. These measure seven feet long by three feet broad and eight feet high, and were not quite dark. They are very rarely occupied, at any

---

* See Appendix A 3.

rate while I was on board. The hospital, a large deck-house situated aft, appeared to be as well arranged and looked after as other parts of the ship, also the smaller "lazaret" for infectious cases, which was empty. There were seven patients in the larger ward, and but one death had occurred throughout the voyage. Ivanoff concluded his rounds by an inspection of the guard—sixty-eight picked sailors from the Imperial Navy, well-built, wiry-looking fellows, armed with the "Berdan" rifle, revolvers, and cutlasses.

"Eleven of these are on duty at a time, night and day," said Ivanoff, a remark that led me to inquire whether their number was not rather inadequate to the large number of convicts.

"Would they be enough in case of mutiny?" I asked as we reached the upper deck, where Captain Ostolopoff was reclining on a deck chair, his huge boarhound "Yashka" basking in the sunshine at his feet.

"There is no such word as mutiny on board my ship, Mr. De Windt," said the captain, whose quick ear had caught the last word; "and I will tell you why," pointing to a large

A RUNAWAY CONVICT, ISLE OF SAKHALIN.

brass-nozzled hose trained against the starboard bulwarks. "There are four of those—one at every corner of the upper deck—leading direct from the engine-room. A turn of the wrist, and in an instant the lower decks and every 'Kamera' would be swept clear of every living being. Steam and boiling water are better than powder and shot. They don't spoil my decks, and are quite as effective! No, we've never *had* a mutiny," added Ostolopoff, lighting another cigarette, "and so long as our friends below are aware of this simple little contrivance, I don't think we ever shall!"

At this moment the pretty, dark-eyed young woman I have spoken of appeared on deck. She had lost some of her shyness, and as we had already conversed that morning, I laughingly repeated the captain's remark for her benefit. As I spoke, however, a glance from Ivanoff warned me too late that I had said the wrong thing, and I cursed my carelessness as the girl, flushing brightly, turned on her heel and walked aft. Nor did I realise the gravity of the *faux pas* I had committed until some time after, for Ivanoff was evidently unwilling to enlighten me, and I did not like to press the matter. But it was she who freely forgave me when, a few days later, I heard from her own lips the true facts of her strange romantic story.

"How could you know?" she said, with a

CONVICT TYPES.

shrug of her pretty shoulders. "Such things only happen in Russia!"

The days on board the *Yaroslav* passed pleasantly enough, and deliciously warm, bright weather favoured the first portion of our voyage. The library contained plenty of books, and there were always cards or music to while away the evenings and lazier hours of the day. I often tried, during the long sunny mornings, to get a snap-shot of the convicts at exercise; but at first sight of the "Kodak" they invariably turned away in a body, notwithstanding the good-humoured remonstrances of the guards. The illustrations on pages 11 and 13 are from Government photographs, as are most of the others depicting convict life. They do not depict the Russian criminal in a very favourable light; but, although there were some truly diabolical countenances on the *Yaroslav*, the remembrance of which was somewhat disquieting on stormy nights, the majority of the faces I saw were rather stolidly stupid than ill-favoured. Some there were of good birth and superior education, and these one could tell at a glance from the old jail-birds, who were some of them returning for the third or fourth time to Sakhalin. Close observation throughout the voyage convinced me that ill-usage of convicts by the guards is very unusual, for the simple reason that it is invariably reported and severely

CONVICT TYPES.

punished. For instance, a warder would at once be dismissed from his post for striking a prisoner. It is not jailers, but prison mates, that the Siberian convict has to fear, especially if he be of timid disposition or feeble frame, and many a lad whose first offence would probably have been his last, enters the prison hold to leave it morally and physically ruined by the terrible experiences he has undergone. A case of this kind came under my own observation on board the *Yaroslav*. It was my custom to smoke a cigar after dinner at sunset on the upper deck, and look down into the brightly lit holds during the hour before evening prayer. On one occasion a group of men gathered around a recumbent figure attracted my attention. Suspecting a case of illness, I summoned Ivanoff, who stealthily approached the spot and watched closely for a few moments. Then the whole truth was revealed. It transpired that a young fellow of weak intellect had, for some trifling offence, complained of one of his companions. Burning for revenge, the latter had reported him to the "Starosta"* or head-man of his

---

* The "Starosta" is himself a convict, elected by his fellow prisoners.

gang, who, as the offence was in his eyes a very serious one, sentenced him "to be kept

CONVICT TYPES.

awake for seven consecutive days and nights." This was now being done, every man taking a watch of two hours after nightfall. An inquiry led to the severe punishment of all and the removal of the victim, a thin, pale-faced lad of about eighteen, to the infirmary; but this instance will show how the most fiendish cruelties may be carried on under the very nose of the authorities, and how extremely difficult it is to check them. Had not Ivanoff's practised eye lit upon their proceedings, these human devils would probably have carried out their plan to the bitter end, for, to a casual observer, they were merely indulging in rough horseplay. At night the unhappy wretch was kept awake by pins thrust into his arms and legs, but like hundreds of others, he dared not complain for fear of being subjected to still greater tortures. I merely quote this case as one of personal experience. It becomes insignificant when compared with other cases of cruelty by convicts that have come under my notice in Siberia.

Nearing Sakhalin, we ran into a succession of thick fogs very prevalent in these regions, and which, unlike most fogs, are often accompanied by violent gales and a heavy sea. Navigation at such times is both difficult and dangerous, while the changes of temperature are remarkable. I have known the thermometer in these regions to fall from 54° to 30° Fahr. in less than two hours. During dirty weather my cramped quarters on the *Yaroslav* were anything but desirable, especially at night-time. Even sea-sickness — to which he was a martyr — did not deter the little " Kapellmeister " from rendering night hideous with his favourite instrument, the clarionet, and I was only consoled on these occasions by the fact that the fog-horn immediately overhead would, under any circumstances, have successfully murdered sleep. I do not know which was worse — the shriek of the steam-syren, or my companion's rendering of " Ta-ra-ra-boom-de-ay," an air of which he was particularly fond.

Our cabin was barely large enough for the accommodation of one medium-sized man, but, fortunately for myself, the musician's personal baggage was extremely limited. It consisted of a mysterious brown-paper parcel (contents unknown), a broken comb, and a brand-new uniform. No schoolgirl was ever prouder of her first ball-dress than my little friend of his regimentals, which I once caught him trying on in the middle of the night. He was, he informed me, the first bandmaster ever sent to Sakhalin, and I cannot help thinking that, if the inhabitants are gifted with a taste for music, he will be the last. But the band was, it appeared, only in "embryo," so perhaps they were spared after all. Poor little Kapellmeister! He was the butt of the ship, but universally popular, if only for the amusement he unconsciously afforded, although, to do him justice, he played the violin divinely. The mysterious young lady, Mademoiselle Elnikoff, was even better on the piano, and my pleasantest evenings on the *Yaroslav* are associated with the strains of *Cavalleria Rusticana*, and the strange, weird melodies of Moskovsky and Glinka, melodies so typical of the great mysterious land that gave them birth.

CHAPTER III.

"OLGA."*

EVERYBODY on board, even the "Kapellmeister," called her by her Christian name. Although I did not, at the time, presume so far as to follow the general example, I will, for the sake of brevity, do so now. Every one, also, from "Yashka," the old boar-hound, upwards, loved her for her comely little face, sweet disposition, and pretty, naïve manner, contrasting so strangely with the brave, self-reliant nature and act of noble self-sacrifice that had brought her amongst us. A history such as Olga Elnikoff's is, in these practical *fin de siècle* days, rarely met with out of the pages of a three-volume novel,

---

* The names of the persons mentioned in this sketch are fictitious.

and I cannot do better than give it as it fell from her own lips.

It was past midnight. The air was motionless, and a myriad stars shone on the glassy surface of the sea, which washed past our quarter as silently as quicksilver, and rippled in our wake like a babbling stream. The shadowy figures of the sentries on the lower deck, and the officer of the watch, as he rapidly paced the bridge, were alone visible when I found myself, for the first time, alone with Olga Elnikoff. That something had gone wrong that day was very evident by the changed manner of my little friend, usually so bright and cheerful, now so *distraite* and depressed, and I ventured to inquire the cause. She was silent for a few moments, and then, in her pretty, impulsive way, replied :

"You are pretty sure to hear all about it sooner or later. I would sooner you heard the true facts from me. But you write—and I was afraid you would publish names which would give pain to my poor old mother in Russia. I would otherwise have told you long ago, for

I have been afraid of your hearing some garbled version of the affair. Tell me: can I trust you to conceal the identity of every one concerned in it?"

I gladly gave the required promise, also assuring Olga that, should she prefer it, I would never publish a word of her story. She merely objected, however, to the disclosure of names, and I therefore have no scruples in placing it before the reader.

Olga Elnikoff was born in the city of Moscow in the year 1870. Of noble birth, much of her girlhood was passed in Paris, Nice, and other Continental resorts generally affected by Russians of the wealthier class, who seem occasionally possessed with a mania for living anywhere but in their own country. Olga was an only child, and was, as a natural consequence, idolised by her father and mother, whose reckless indulgence would have spoiled a less lovable nature. But Olga, even at an early age, had developed qualities that might have served as an example to her parents, neither

D

of whom was overburdened with either common sense or firmness. Many a young and thoughtless girl would have become demoralised by the artificial, unwholesome atmosphere by which she was generally surrounded; the eternal round of gaiety, only dropped at one place to be resumed at another, the feverish, frivolous existence of Russo-American society on the Riviera and elsewhere; but although the pleasures of life were by no means thrown away upon Olga's gay, vivacious temperament, she managed, somehow, to find time for more serious pursuits. The intellectual part of her education was, therefore, not entirely neglected, though this was chiefly due to herself, her parents being on this point as careless and indifferent as they were lavish in their love and affection for the daughter who, from babyhood upwards, had never expressed a wish that was not immediately granted.

So the years slipped happily away, until the cloud, destined for ever to darken Olga's future, appeared on the fair horizon of her life.

The Elnikoffs were wintering in Rome, and

it was after a ball given on the occasion of his daughter's twentieth birthday that Count Elnikoff complained of slight indisposition. Two days later typhoid fever of a malignant type had declared itself, and within a week Olga was fatherless. A distant cousin, upon whom the dead man had never set eyes, succeeded to the family estates, which were entailed. The Count had left a will bequeathing personal property of considerable value to his wife and daughter; but the careless, light-hearted Russian was never remarkable for business qualities. His extravagance was proverbial, and he was a gambler. The outside world was, therefore, not so surprised as it might have been to hear that Count Elnikoff was, at the time of his death, hopelessly involved, and that Olga and her mother were, if not actually paupers, sufficiently reduced in circumstances to merit the name in the eyes of society.

Adversity is a powerful antidote to grief, and although prostrated for a few days by the terrible loss she had sustained, Olga soon began to realise that one cannot, in this world at least, live upon air, and that to keep the wolf from the door, something must be done without delay. The sum saved from the wreck amounted to 50,000 roubles, or about £5,000. This, she pointed out to her mother, would enable them both to return to Russia, and settle in some University town, where Olga could pursue her studies under the cheapest and most favourable circumstances, for a year. This would fit her for the post of governess, either in Russia or abroad; and although Countess Elnikoff was at first repelled by the idea of such a menial situation, she was at length forced to admit that there was no alternative. Kharkoff was therefore chosen as a residence, and less than six weeks after her father's death found Olga Elnikoff and her mother installed in a cheap quarter of the University town.

Eager to carry out her scheme, Olga awaited with impatience the conclusion of the Christmas festival and reassemblage of the University. It was dreary, uphill work at first, and it severely tried Olga's courage and fortitude to plod through the hard, thankless tasks that were, after all, only preparing her for a life of still greater toil and drudgery. There were days, too—gray, wintry days—when the contrast between the sunny, pleasant times by the blue Mediterranean and the uneventful monotony of her present existence would present itself so vividly, that the poor child would throw down her work in despair, only to resume it the next moment with the reflection that every day cost money, and that she must no longer encroach upon her mother's slender store. And, with ever-increasing anxiety, Countess Elnikoff watched the pale, anxious face and weary eyes, that told of long, harassing days and nights of work and worry, but remonstrated with her daughter in vain.

Olga made but few acquaintances at Kharkoff, although some of the classes were attended by many students of both sexes; but Olga held aloof as far as possible from casual companionship, with one exception. This was Mitza

Lepsky, a quiet, ladylike girl from Wilna, with whom Olga one day formed an acquaintance that soon ripened into close friendship. Countess Elnikoff welcomed the girl warmly, for it seemed to put new life into her daughter to have some one of her own world to associate with, and Mitza Lepsky, although poor, was vastly superior in every way to the majority of the students who attended the schools. There was much in common, too, between Olga and her new friend, for the Polish girl's father had been wealthy until ruined by the failure of a Vienna bank. Mitza had but one relative in the world — a brother studying medicine at Kieff University, who, upon the occasion of a visit to his sister at Kharkoff, was presented to the Elnikoffs.

Serge Lepsky was about twenty-five years of age, and by no means handsome. He was not even attractive to the few women with whom he came in contact; but his pleasant manners and low, musical voice charmed Olga, who instinctively contrasted the owner with the rowdy, cigarette-smoking youths she was in the habit of meeting during work hours. There was something strange, too, about him, and women love mystery. She infinitely preferred him, after a time, to any of the men she had known in happier days — idle, vacuous creatures for the most part, with ideas bounded by their tailor and the latest scandal, who had never succeeded in inspiring any feeling but one of amusement in the mind of this wayward Russian girl, who, ever since she left her cradle, had never learned the real meaning of the word love.

Serge Lepsky, also, for the first time in his life, felt strangely attracted by Olga's vivid personality, her self-abnegation and devotion to her mother. He was a worker who, up till now, had given little heed to the opposite sex; but Olga was a revelation in womankind. So Kieff was deserted for a time, and Kharkoff became Serge's headquarters, much to his sister's amusement, for Mitza had always looked upon her brother as a confirmed misogynist, quite impervious to feminine attractions. Then, as if in compensation for the dark days she had passed through, succeeded the happiest time that Olga had ever known, culminating on the day that she promised to marry the man who had become as necessary to her existence as the breath of life itself. Although barely six months had elapsed since their first meeting, Countess Elnikoff had entire confidence in Lepsky, and gladly gave her consent to the wedding, which it was arranged should take place as soon as possible. Meanwhile, Serge would not hear of the carrying out of Olga's scheme. This, he insisted, must be at once abandoned, for he was possessed of sufficient means to enable him to take out his diploma, and afterwards set up in practice—if possible in Kharkoff, so that, as he jokingly said, the Countess should never have cause to regret the match, which at one time looked so full of hope and happiness, but which was fated to have such an unexpected and terrible ending.

- One bright summer morning, early in June of 1893, Olga took leave of her lover at the Kharkoff railway station. It was necessary that he should return to Kieff in order to take leave of his professors and settle up his private affairs. This would occupy at most three days, at the expiration of which he intended to rejoin his *fiancée*, who was very much averse to even this short separation. But Serge faithfully promised to write often, and to return to the minute on the appointed day. Besides, they were to be married in ten days; so that, when the train had disappeared, Olga left the platform with a light heart to impatiently await the following morning, which would not only hasten the happy event by a day, but also bring a letter from her lover. Every day brought news of the absent one; but the third morning a bitter disappointment was in store. Urgent business, the writer said, necessitated his remaining in Kieff for at least two days longer. The letter was written in a careless, hurried strain, very unlike Serge's usual, precise, methodical style, which at first caused Olga some anxiety; but Mitza reassured her. Serge was, no doubt, busy himself about the diploma, she said, and as the formalities to be gone through were endless, the delay was only natural. But the next morning no letter at all was forthcoming, and Olga, after a day passed in worry and suspense, was beginning to be seriously alarmed when, at dusk, just as her mother and Mitza were sitting down to supper, Serge himself appeared. He looked tired and pale, Olga thought, and his hand shook as he hastily filled and drank off a liqueur-glass of vodka, so the girl spared him the reproaches which rose to her lips. Poor fellow, something had evidently worried him terribly, so she mentally resolved to ask no questions until the morning, although at first his strange, unusual appearance almost frightened her into so doing. His dress, usually so neat, was dusty and disordered, and there were lines about his mouth and eyes that she had never noticed before. He looked ten years older. During supper, however, Serge brightened up somewhat, and when Olga, at his request, had seated herself at the piano, he had almost recovered his usual spirit.

It was nearly eleven o'clock. The Countess was engaged in some intricate embroidery, Mitza was reading by the light of a shaded lamp, and strains of Mendelssohn's "Lieder ohne Wörte," played just loud enough to drown the conversation by the piano, filled the apartment with dreamy, sensuous music, when a loud knock at the outer door, followed by a confused murmur of voices, brought Serge to his feet with an oath. The women looked blankly at each other with pale, startled faces, as he held up a finger to enjoin silence.

There was a dead stillness for a few moments, broken only by the tick of a clock on the whitewashed wall, and the distant roar of the city. Olga looked inquiringly at Serge, whose face had grown livid. Regardless of his warning, she was about to speak, when again interrupted by a loud rap that threatened to smash the flimsy woodwork. Then a voice rang out clear on the still night air: "Open, in the name of the Tzar."

"Stay, I will go," said Serge, brushing

hastily past his sister, who was moving toward the door. He opened it, passed across the little vestibule, and, drawing aside the bolts, threw open the outer door. As he did so, the soft lamplight from the sitting-room shone faintly on silver accoutrements and black and yellow facings. The dimly lit landing was filled with men. Olga knew them only too well. It was the police.

Closing the door behind him, Serge returned to the apartment, followed by a stout, gray-bearded little man, beaming through an enormous pair of spectacles—the Chief of Police. Glancing quickly around, the latter uncovered, and, addressing Serge, muttered in an undertone:

"You had better get these women away."

Receiving no reply, he produced, with a shrug of his round shoulders, a document which he slowly proceeded to unfold, shifting his gaze the while from one to the other of the silent, terror-stricken women. Then, advancing to the lamp, he examined the page for a few moments, and continued:

"Serge Alexandrovitch Lepsky, I arrest you on suspicion of murdering Otto Heinrich Peltzer at the village of Oulnik, in the province of Kieff, on the afternoon of the 12th of May, 1891."

But Olga was happily spared the harrowing details that followed, for, when Serge was removed in custody, a dead swoon had already rendered ·the poor child unconscious of her surroundings.

The chain of evidence produced at the trial left no room for doubt as to Serge Lepsky's guilt, although the apparent absence of motive presented the most curious feature of this mysterious affair. Peltzer was the only fellow student with whom Serge had been on terms of anything like intimacy; for the latter's quiet, reserved nature had seldom led him into society of any kind, and he had not a dozen acquaintances in the whole University. It was proved that, on the day of the murder (the day before his return to Kharkoff), Serge and his friend had set out with their rods for Oulnik, a small village about twenty miles from Kieff, much frequented by anglers for its excellent trout-fishing. After partaking of refreshment at the village inn, they had started at midday for the riverside, and nothing more was afterwards seen of them. Two shots were heard during the afternoon by peasants working near the river; but the place being a favourite resort of sportsmen, no notice was taken of the occurrence. Towards evening, the body of Peltzer was found lying on its face, with two bullet wounds in the back, and the throat cut from ear to ear. At the same time chance led to the recovery of a six-chambered revolver, which had probably been hastily thrown into the river, but which had lodged in the mud, just clear of the water. Only two of the chambers, which had all been loaded, had been discharged. It was therefore surmised that the assassin, fearing that the firing might attract attention, had finished his ghastly work with a knife or razor, which, however, was never found. The dead man's watch, rings, and money were untouched, which at once disposed of the theory of robbery; but suspicion would, under any circumstances, have fallen on Lepsky, who was observed, the same morning, leaving the city with his friend. Nor did the former attempt to deny his guilt. "I did it," he said simply. "He deserved his fate;" and neither entreaties nor threats could elicit a single word more. The plea of insanity, put in as a last resource, was finally abandoned, and as there is no capital punishment, except for regicide, in Russia, Serge Lepsky was sentenced to deportation for life to the Island of Sakhalin.

The interest attaching to this *cause célèbre* was not confined to Kharkoff, but extended throughout European Russia. Most of the leading newspapers devoted columns to the elucidation of the mystery, but without success. It is a significant fact, however, that although Olga Elnikoff had at first, like the rest of the world, turned with repulsion from one who had been suddenly transformed into an inhuman fiend, she eventually returned from a private interview, earnestly begged for by the convict, firmly resolved to accompany her affianced husband into exile. Through the intervention of a Grand Duchess, whom Olga had known in brighter days, special permission was granted her to travel in the same ship as Serge Lepsky, and to marry him immediately on arrival at Sakhalin. By the same influence she was appointed Government Schoolmistress at Alexandrovsky-Post until her husband should, at the expiration of five years, regain his provisional liberty.

Were this a novel, I should certainly clear up the story by making Serge Lepsky the avenging agent of a secret society, and, as Kieff University is noted for its Socialistic tendencies, this appears to me the most likely solution of the mystery. But this is sheer supposition on my part, for the crime may have been prompted by entirely private motives, the more so that, had Lepsky ever dabbled in politics, he would probably have come under the notice of the Secret Police. Under any circumstances, Olga Elnikoff's renewed loyalty and devotion point to the possibility of either great provocation, or pressure from some unseen power; but the dark secret, divulged to her by Serge, will assuredly be buried with them both on that lonely island in the North Pacific Ocean.

Day was breaking as Olga concluded her story, and the coast of Sakhalin was already visible, like a great black snake asleep upon the gray, dawn-lit sea.

"You have not yet told me your trouble," I said, as with a yawn and a shiver my little friend gave a careless glance at her new home, and turned to go below. "Is there anything I can do to help you?" I asked, as we walked slowly towards the companion.

"He was in punishment to-day," she whispered after a pause, with averted face, "and, for the first time since leaving Odessa, I have not been permitted to see him."

CHAPTER IV.

THE ISLAND OF SAKHALIN (KORSAKOVSKY-POST).

KAMCHATKA is, by its very remoteness, almost a household word in England, and although it would no doubt puzzle many of my readers to accurately locate that dreary peninsula, I fancy there are many more who have never even heard of the adjacent Island of Sakhalin, which, like a huge centipede, sprawls parallel with the coast of Siberia from the north of Yezo to the Sea of Okhotsk.

Sakhalin is by no means easy of access at any time, and during the greater part of the year is quite unapproachable by water. With the exception of a small coasting steamer and two or three sealing schooners, the vessels of the Russian Volunteer Fleet are the only ones that visit the island with any regularity during the short summer season, which lasts from the end of May until the middle of October. Even then landing is not always possible for many days after arrival, for although possessed of a

DOG-POST—SAKHALIN TO EUROPE. "ON THE ROAD."

coast line of over twelve hundred miles, Sakhalin has not a single harbour worthy of the name. During the winter the island is completely shut in by ice, and communication with the mainland is then kept up viâ Nikolaefsk by means of dog-sledges across the frozen straits of Tartary, which are here about eight miles wide. Although half the island as far back as 1857 was claimed by Russia, who commenced landing convicts there in 1869, Sakhalin originally belonged to the Japanese, who only formally ceded it (in exchange for the Kurile Islands) in 1875.

At midday on the tenth day after leaving Nagasaki, we anchored off the settlement of Korsakovsky-Post. We had closely skirted the coast ever since entering the narrow straits of La Perouse at an early hour that morning, and I must own to a feeling of agreeable disappointment at my first glimpse of the New Siberia, which upon closer acquaintance presented anything but a gloomy or depressing appearance, though perhaps the glorious weather and pure exhilarating air had something to do with it. Tiny fishing villages became visible, dotted here and there along the coast, imparting an air of life and animation to the well-wooded shores. Inland a succession of snowy peaks glittered against a sky of cloudless blue, while the sea sparkled with Mediterranean brilliancy in the morning sunshine. The swift current that runs through the narrow passage between the islands of Yezo and Sakhalin somewhat retarded our progress, but two o'clock saw us anchored off Korsakovsky-Post. As no prisoners are landed here our stay was likely to be a short one, so I made arrangements with the Governor, who boarded us immediately on arrival, to visit the prison early next morning.

Five thousand criminal convicts are located at Korsakovsky-Post, but of these only about twelve hundred are actually under lock and key. The settlement, which stands in a valley formed by, on the one side, precipitous pine-clad cliffs, and on the other by bleak-looking sand-dunes extending for some distance inland, consists of one long straggling thoroughfare, which, commencing at the landing-stage, is brought to an abrupt termination at the summit of the steep hill by the chief feature in the landscape, a huge prison, the grim gray walls and barred windows of which blur the skyline, and cast a gloomy shadow over the pretty gardens and neat whitewashed log huts which are occupied by prison officials, and line the main street.

I was struck next morning with the cheerful aspect of this place when compared with other towns and settlements in Siberia. This is probably owing to the lighter colour of the soil and whitewashed buildings, which lend a gaiety to the landscape never met with on the mainland, where the universal drab of earth and dwelling is usually unrelieved by any brighter colouring than the varied shades of vegetation, sombre for the most part. On landing we were met by the Governor, who invited us to his house prior to visiting the prison. At the landing-stage a couple of hundred convicts were engaged rolling away the stores left by the *Yaroslav* along a tramway to the land end of the pier. Here another gang were stationed to receive and carry them up to the general storehouse, a large wooden building a few hundred yards distant. The main street presented a certain amount of activity, and, to a stranger, the casual way in which people in prison garb were strolling about at their avocations alone and unattended was at first, to say the least of it, surprising. I saw few women, but many respectable-looking, decently-dressed men, apparently of the artisan class, who, without exception, respectfully saluted us. I ascribed this at first to the presence of the Governor, but the same thing occurring when I returned alone to the ship in the evening, I made inquiry, and found that these men were free colonists who had completed their terms of hard labour. Many of them appeared so refined in manners and appearance that their ultra-respectful demeanour at first astonished me, but I soon learnt that one may take it as a general rule that, on Sakhalin, if a man is not an official he is, or has been, a convict.

A walk of five minutes up the well-kept street, with its neat wooden pavements and oil street lamps, past the barracks and pretty green-roofed church, brings us to the Governor's house, a fair-sized building surrounded by verandas and a spacious garden, the internal arrangements of which are very different to what

I had expected to find. Indeed, the Governor's *ménage* far excelled anything of the kind I had ever seen east of the Urals. The dining-room into which we were shown was a pretty, cheerful apartment, with French windows opening on to the garden. Costly skins littered the mirror-like *parquet* of delicate mosaic, wrought in woods from the forests of the interior. Russian and Turkish embroideries concealed the whitewashed walls, and a beautiful palm in a far corner spread its branches over a grand piano, while, to complete this picture of refinement and luxury, we were received by Madame Vologdine and her pretty little girl at a snowy table where, amid freshly-cut flowers, a dainty *déjeuner* awaited us. The repast was prepared by a gentleman from Odessa, who had deprived an aged and wealthy relative of existence under circumstances of peculiar atrocity, but I am bound to admit that this fact did not lessen either my appetite, or appreciation of a certain delicious "omelette soufflée," which yet lingers in my memory.

It was very hot. The venetians were closely drawn to exclude the dazzling sunshine, and a buzz of insects filled the air. My hosts were clothed in a manner more suggestive of tropical than northern climes, an opinion I ventured to express during breakfast; but the words were scarcely out of my mouth when the sunlight faded away, the room darkened, and shadows gathered as if night had fallen. All this had occurred with the sudden rapidity of a theatrical transformation scene. "You spoke too soon, you see," laughed Monsieur Vologdine, drawing up the blind, and disclosing a thick, impenetrable fog that would not have disgraced London in late November. Meanwhile, indoors, the air felt perceptibly cooler. These dense fogs are one of the chief drawbacks of Sakhalin, and, except in the interior,-are common throughout the year. They occurred nearly every day during my stay on the island, but usually passed away in a couple of hours.

Although the bright but brief summer on Sakhalin is pleasant enough, the severity of the climate has, up till now, seriously interfered with the development of the physical resources of the island, which would, under any other circumstances, be considerable. Winter lasts from the end of September until the beginning of May, and during this period, outdoor work of every kind is practically at a standstill. The yearly average temperature of Alexandrovsky-Post is only 33° Fahr., and a few years ago, at the neighbouring village of Dui, the Russian explorer Polyakoff found the soil frozen at a depth of thirty-one inches in mid-June, while the snow lay deep on the hills around the settlement.

The sun was once more shining brightly when, after breakfast, we set out with our host for the prison, only a stone's throw distant. It may be well, before visiting this establishment, to briefly explain the various grades of punishment undergone by those sentenced by the Russian Government to deportation by sea.

The criminal convicts on the Island of Sakhalin may be classed under three heads, viz.:

(1) Those who have served their time in prison, and are free to wander at will over a specified district, earning their own living;

(2) Those who are actually confined in prison and work at a trade; and

(3) Those (the dangerous class) who are confined in prison under restraint (viz., manacled or chained to wheelbarrows).

Every convict is placed, on arrival, in Class 2. From this grade he may, by industry and good behaviour, rise in time to Class 1, but he may also, if of an idle and vicious disposition, be relegated to Class 3. Every chance is, however, given him, for unless the offence be unpardonable, it is, as a rule, punished as lightly as circumstances will permit. There is also a graduated scale of what are called remitted sentences. It would weary the reader to enumerate them in detail. Suffice it to say that a man with a life sentence need never pass more than eight years actually in prison, and so on.

Many of the first, or privileged classes, occupy positions as Government clerks, and earn as much as forty-five roubles a month. Others find employment as domestic servants, watchmen, or storekeepers, or by working at the trade they have been brought up to, or learned while in prison. The majority, however, prefer to take advantage of the grant of land made to every convict on his release from captivity, and earn a living by the production of cereal or vegetable produce. In this case a sum of money is advanced by the Government for the purchase of agricultural implements. These loans discharged convicts are expected to repay by small monthly instalments; and it is only fair to add that, in most cases, this compact is faithfully carried out.

The privileges of a well-behaved convict on Sakhalin are no doubt great, but, on the other hand, the punishments meted out to mutinous characters and transgressors of the law are terribly severe. On these occasions the dreaded "Plet," the dark cell, and wheelbarrow are brought into requisition, but of these I shall have something to say later on. The frequency of crime, especially of murder, on the island a few years since, rendered it absolutely necessary to resort to capital punishment as a deterrent. Sakhalin is, therefore, the only place throughout the Russian Empire where the death penalty is now carried out. It is a very necessary precaution, for only a few days before my arrival at Korsakovsky a Japanese storekeeper was murdered in broad daylight while standing in front of his house in the main street of the settlement.

The prison of Korsakovsky-Post consists of a succession of buildings laid out in an oblong, the blocks at either extremity containing kitchens, bakery, storehouses, and workshops, while the side-buildings, of which there are seven, are used as "Kameras." The unpaved yard is a hundred yards in length by thirty yards wide, the whole space being enclosed within a high palisade, which, like the rest of the buildings, is of dingy, unpainted wood, much dilapidated by age and climate. The entrance gates are anything but suggestive of a prison, for they are wide open.

With the exception of a sentry—whose attention is so engrossed by a brisk set-to between two curs down the road that he scarcely notices our arrival—there is, apparently, nothing to prevent the inmates of Korsakovsky Prison from calmly walking out of the place, the more so that the " Kamera " doors are none of them secured. I suggest this to Vologdine, who replies: " Quite so, my dear sir, but where are they to go to ? " This unanswerable view of the question had not occurred to me.

The first object that meets the eye upon entering the yard is a gaudily-painted wooden shrine, erected by the convicts in commemoration of the escape of the Tsarevitch from assassination in Japan, during his journey around the world. Crossing the yard, we pass, on our right, a shed containing two fire-engines, which look as smart and workmanlike as new paint and elbow-grease can make them, and enter the kitchen, where our guide insists upon our tasting the soup that is being prepared in a couple of huge coppers for the midday meal.

It is strong, though to my taste very greasy, and contains meat and vegetables. Here and next door, in the bakery, twenty convicts are employed. The bread is brown and rather coarse, but crisp and fresh, and infinitely superior to the watery, doughy stuff served out in the prisons of Paris. Judging from what I know of these institutions (and I have seen them all), their *habitués* would vastly prefer confinement in Korsakovsky, where meat is given twice and fresh fish three times a week.

The "Kameras" differed but little in size and other particulars, so that the description of one may suffice for all. Imagine a lofty whitewashed hall about forty feet long by thirty feet wide, lit by six large barred windows on either side, made so as to open or shut at will of the inmates. Wooden sleeping platforms are fixed around three sides and down the centre of the room, the resting-place of each man being shown by a neatly-rolled mattress. The latter are provided by Government, a special workshop being set apart for their manufacture. A sacred "Ikon" with lighted taper hangs in a corner, while the walls are adorned with cheap prints clipped, for the most part, from illustrated newspapers. The flooring is thickly strewn every day with pine branches, which diffuse a clean, pungent smell, which, with that of tobacco, permeates the whole place. The sanitary arrangements, though necessarily primitive, are practical and effectual, while every "Kamera" is warmed in winter by a huge stove. The first ward we visited contained thirty-two men, most of whom were smoking, others idling about, for it was their day off work. All were well clothed and appeared in good health. About a third wore chains. As we left two convicts entered with smoking mess-tins of the soup we had tasted, and a huge pail of "Kvas,"* which is provided every Saint's Day in place of the cold water generally supplied.

We visited every "Kamera" in turn. Some were full, others only partly so, others quite empty, their inmates being out at work, wood-

---

* "Kvas" is a beverage made of black rye-bread and mint.

cutting, road-making, and the like. A careful inspection of the Korsakovsky prison convinced me that, so far as regards discipline, cleanliness, and order it needs little improvement. The entire absence of over-crowding was also very noticeable after some of my Siberian experiences.

Only one "Kamera" was set apart for women. It differed little from that of the men, excepting that bedsteads were provided. These prisoners were mostly of the peasant class—blowsy, robust-looking creatures for the most part, with but scanty good looks to atone for lack of intellect. Women are invariably placed in what is called the "Free Class" on arrival at Sakhalin, and are seldom actually incarcerated at all, save for offences committed on the island. On this occasion I found only eight undergoing imprisonment, and none of these wore prison dress. The majority were in for minor offences, the most serious offender being a young girl who had murdered her illegitimate child. For this she had been sentenced to six months' imprisonment, now nearly expired. This "Kamera" smelt close and stuffy, and not nearly as sweet and pure as those of the men, but this was probably due to the absence of pine boughs and tobacco smoke. The walls were bare, but the terms of imprisonment are usually so short, that female convicts do not care to take the trouble to embellish them. While on this subject, I may mention that a law has lately been passed in Russia totally abolishing the whipping of women, either here or on the mainland, under any circumstances.

As I purpose to minutely describe the principal penal establishment of Alexandrovsky-Post, space will not admit of the description of other portions of this prison. The workshops, however, deserve notice, for they were far ahead of anything I had pictured as being possible in this mushroom settlement. I must have traversed at least a dozen large sheds where work was in full swing. The smithy was perhaps the best. Here they were putting the finishing touches to a very creditable "Tarantass," entirely built in the prison, and commencing on a pair of ornamental iron altar-screens for the church. Shoemaking, tailoring, carpentering, even the use of the lathe and wood-carving, all these are taught in Korsakovsky Prison, and so far with admirable results. The workshops were old, tumble-down buildings, scarcely weatherproof; but new ones, which we visited, are in course of construction.

The school founded for the children of prisoners by Madame Pobodonostzeff and other ladies of St. Petersburg is within the prison *enceinte*, and is in every way admirably conducted, and I am glad to be able to state, from personal experience and observation, that there are few large prisons in Russia without an institution of this kind. It was also more than satisfactory, after all the rubbish anent the treatment of the sick in Siberian prisons that has been published in England, to visit the infirmary, where the light, airy wards, well-tended sick, and well-stocked pharmacy, would have satisfied even an English physician. The hospital has eighty beds, but contained only twenty-seven patients, the majority of whom were suffering from pulmonary diseases and rheumatism. Perhaps the saddest sight in this place was a poor fellow who had been here three years, and who, with a suddenness that startled me, thrust a paper into my hands, which he implored me to hand to the Governor of Vladivostok. His hallucination was that it contained the disclosure of a plot to assassinate the Tzar.

The Governor's carriage was awaiting us outside the prison, a vehicle closely resembling an Irish jaunting-car, drawn by a pair of well-shaped, high-spirited ponies, who dashed into their collars, galloped down the street, and whisked around the corner at the bottom of the hill with a rapidity that nearly shot me into the road. Horses were unknown in Sakhalin until twenty years ago, when they were first imported from Siberia, and now thrive remarkably well. Our destination was a village three miles distant, rejoicing in the Neapolitan-sounding name of Por-na-maré, an Ainu word signifying

"Lost-in-the-marsh," and the road to which is cut through dense, impenetrable forest. A drive of about a quarter of an hour over rocks, ruts, and rotten bridges that threw us about like peas in a baby's rattle, and threatened to tear the carriage in half, brought us to the village, a collection of log huts situated close to the seashore. As we approached, the howling of dogs attracted my attention, and I then discovered that the canine population far exceeded the number of human inhabitants, for here, as in regions further North, the sleigh dog plays a very important rôle. Every dwelling was surrounded by them, while long strings of fish dangled in the sunshine drying for their consumption in the winter-time. They were snarling, savage-looking brutes, and I should not have cared to walk through the place alone after dark.

Por-na-maré is a long, straggling village. Its population numbers under one hundred, and consists almost exclusively of time-expired convicts. A good deal of the land around is under cultivation, chiefly of garden produce, although rye and barley, I was told, did well, though of rather poor quality. On the other hand, potatoes, cabbages, and other roots grew luxuriantly. Most of the dwellings were closed, the owners being at work on their land, but we entered one of the huts, that of a Finn, who was living with a Polish woman who had poisoned her husband in Russia. She was a bright, good-looking young woman, dressed in neat pink cotton, with the clearest blue eyes I have ever seen, and undoubtedly an excellent housewife, to judge from the conspicuous cleanliness of everything around: the spotless plank floor, the bright copper pans, and snowy window-curtains. The man was a dull, sulky-looking lout, who answered in monosyllables, and left most of the talking to Madame, who, judging from her pretty baby face, did not look capable of wilfully injuring a black-beetle. But experience has taught me that criminal physiognomy is very misleading.

On the way home, a tall, flaxen-haired

individual accosted us and begged for a moment's conversation with Vologdine. The stranger wore a tweed suit and dark wideawake, and looked like a respectable tradesman, which, indeed, he had once been. He was no Russian, Vologdine said, but a German from Königsberg on the Baltic, who had been sent to Sakhalin for forgery. His term had now expired, and he begged to be allowed to return to Europe in the *Yaroslav*, a request which, upon the production of his papers, was at once granted. "But your house," called back Vologdine, as we were driving off. "I have sold it," replied the Teuton, holding up a sheaf of rouble notes with a broad grin on his sunburnt face. Foreigners undergoing sentence on Sakhalin may return to their own country after a residence of five years on the island from the expiration of their term of hard labour. This is not so, however, with Russian subjects, who are only permitted to return to Europe under very exceptional circumstances.

The sun was setting as we drove into Korsakovsky-Post, where I took leave of my host and his family, after thanking the former for his kindness and attention. I returned alone to the ship, declining Borkovsky's invitation to join him in a bear-hunting expedition fourteen versts distant, which, although he remained in the open all night, proved unsuccessful. Stepping on board the *Yaroslav* I was hailed in the English language by two strangers, and was subsequently delighted to find that they were fellow-countrymen, who, in Sakhalin, are about as rare as nuggets in paving-stones. They proved to be Messrs. Denbigh and Graham-Campbell; the former a hale, hearty-looking man of about fifty years of age, and a resident of Sakhalin, the latter a traveller and his guest for the time being. The meeting was opportune, although Mr. Denbigh's account of the interior of the island, which I proposed to visit, was anything but encouraging. The woods, he said, were infested with runaway convicts, who would not scruple to kill a man for a couple of roubles or the clothes he wore. My informant was an old King's College man, who had resided here for over twenty years, and who had visited England only twice in all that period. In order to obtain the monopoly of two hundred miles of coast for fishing purposes, Mr. Denbigh had become a naturalised Russian subject, and now employs over fifteen hundred men, including four hundred convicts. His station, Mauka, is situated one hundred and fifty miles by sea, and eighty miles by land, from Korsakovsky, but the last-mentioned road is only practicable in winter. The majority of the fish are herrings, and an idea may be formed of the quantity caught by the fact that, in two days of 1894, over six thousand tons were landed at Mauka. The fish is sun-dried and shipped off to Japan, where it fetches a good price as manure for the tea-plantations and paddy-fields. The usual price paid on delivery is £8 per ton; but owing to the comparatively small quantity on the market, it frequently rises to £14. A large trade is also done in the long, ribbon-like pieces of seaweed, which are gathered, dried, and shipped to China, where, being considered a great delicacy, they fetch large prices.

Mr. Denbigh also trades largely in skins. This reminds me that, on my departure from England, many of my friends commissioned me to purchase them furs, thinking that I could, no doubt, buy them cheap where they came from. There is no greater mistake than this. In the first place, sable skins, for instance, must be bought by the dozen from the native dealer, without the option of picking out the good ones, which generally leaves a percentage in your favour of one or two, at most, to the twelve. Secondly, they are badly cured, and as stiff as boards. They must consequently be re-dressed; and thirdly, the game is really not worth the candle, for you can buy a first-rate skin of any kind in St. Petersburg or Moscow (I exclude other Continental cities) for at least half the price that you can purchase them here. I bought, some two years ago, a fur coat at Irkoutsk, in Siberia, and found that, though the skins were from a district not a hundred miles distant, they had already travelled to Europe (to be properly dressed) and back again. To say nothing of all these drawbacks, none but those possessed of unlimited wealth should ever attempt to buy "skins in the rough," for it is like gambling—a very expensive amusement in the end.

Like most Englishmen well acquainted with Russia, Mr. Denbigh had little but good to say of the Siberian Exile System, especially regarding Sakhalin, where, he said, the authorities erred, if anything, on the side of leniency. Most of the four hundred convicts in his employ at Mauka were a lazy, good-for-nothing lot, continually grumbling at their pay and fighting with their Japanese fellow-workmen. Mr. Denbigh was strictly forbidden to take the law into his own hands, so that it became at times almost impossible to keep order, and he would often gladly have dispensed altogether with their poor services. This was, however, impossible, the contract engaging them for a stated period.

Our conversation turning upon the credulity of the English and American public where Russian prison affairs are concerned, Mr. Denbigh related an amusing adventure connected with this subject which had befallen him a couple of years previously. A party of ten convicts at Mauka, taking advantage of their absolute liberty, resolved to escape from the island. They appropriated for this purpose a large lighter used for fishing purposes, the property of their employer, and having stocked her with provisions purloined from the storehouse (to which one of them had access), put to sea, and in a few days fell in with an American vessel bound for San Francisco. The usual fables of cruelty and oppression on the part of Russian prison officials were not lost upon the captain, a simple, kindhearted man, who agreed to say nothing about the matter, and to land the men in America. News of this occurrence had not reached Mr. Denbigh (who was in England at the time), when, a few weeks later, passing through San Francisco on his way to Mauka, he read of the escape in a local newspaper. The fugitives had just landed, and five columns were devoted to the "Ten men of Katorga," as they were described by an enthusiastic reporter, who was presumably unaware that "Katorga" is not the name of a place, but signifies, in the Russian language, "hard labour." This, however, is a trifling and harmless error compared to the tissue of falsehoods, connected with Siberian prison life, that followed. A short term of liberty in a civilised city had evidently shown even these illiterate convicts that sensationalism is (in these days, and from a pecuniary point of view) infinitely preferable to truth. But if Mr. Denbigh's former employés were amused (as, indeed, they must have been) at the gullibility of the American journalist who took notes of their fictitious martyrdom, they must have positively roared with laughter when their portraits appeared, with a suitable bordering of knouts and fetters, on the principal page of a leading San Francisco journal.

Hearing that the men were on view at a

Dime Museum not far from his hotel, Mr. Denbigh, much to their consternation, once more confronted his old friends, who were visibly relieved when they found that the unwelcome visitor had no intention of interfering with their operations. Apologising in Russian for the theft of the stores and lighter, their spokesman explained that, being weary of the monotony of life on the island, they had determined to try their luck elsewhere; although, he added patronisingly, they had nothing to say against the treatment they had received while at Mauka. Mr. Denbigh, being well aware that they had led as comfortable an existence as the average English farm labourer, was not so impressed by this admission as he might have been. "But why do you tell such lies about the place?" he asked mildly. "It can do no harm," was the reply, "and interests the people. Many come night and day. We have plenty to eat, drink, and smoke. Oh, it's better than Sakhalin," said the man with a grin, lurching back to his seat on the green-baize platform as the strains of a jingling piano-organ ushered in a fresh batch of admirers.*

With these and other pleasant reminiscences of distant lands we beguiled the hours till midnight, when my countrymen left us to board the little sealing schooner that was to bear them back, at daylight, to Mauka. The latter is from all accounts pleasant enough as a summer residence, but it must in winter-time present a truly desolate appearance.

I retired to rest well pleased with my day's work, for I must own that I had approached Sakhalin expecting to find, if not actually horrors, a very different state of things to that existing in Western Siberia. The scanty information I had been able to glean was chiefly of the "hearsay" order, and my search for modern works of travel bearing on the subject had proved quite fruitless. Novels there were, and

---

* Of the "Ten men of Katorga," five were imprisoned for various offences within six months of their arrival in San Francisco, while a short time ago a sixth was tried and executed for murder in the same city. (See Appendix E.)

by the score, minutely describing life—especially prison life—on the island. One of these works of fiction especially had inspired me with grave misgivings, for it was written as by one having authority. "The Inferno of Sakhalin," it said, "has no parallel in human nature. It is the gate of an Eternal Hell."*

Let us charitably assume that the writer is personally unacquainted with the island he so graphically describes.

---

* "The Princess of Alaska," by Col. R. H. Savage.

CHAPTER V.

THE ISLAND OF SAKHALIN (ALEXANDROVSKY-POST).

THE Island of Sakhalin is, or was at the time of my visit, governed by His Excellency General Merkazine, who resided at Alexandrovsky-Post, which is therefore the chief town or settlement. The prison here is precisely similar to the prison of Korsakovsky-Post as regards general administration, but the convicts, instead of, as at the latter place, working in the fields, are chiefly employed in foundries and workshops, of which there are a considerable number. A telegraph wire now connects Alexandrovsky-Post with the mainland of Siberia, and every penal settlement on Sakhalin, which circumstance has greatly reduced the number of escapes.

We anchored off the town at midday, and

the landing of the prisoners commenced shortly afterwards. This was rapidly effected, for the sea was as smooth as glass, but stormy weather occasionally causes a delay of two or three days, for the roadstead is quite unprotected, and a heavy sea sometimes renders the passage of a mile or so not only difficult but dangerous. The boats used to convey the prisoners ashore somewhat resemble coal-barges of deep draught, and are capable of carrying ninety men at a time. Four of these were loaded simultaneously, two aft and two forward, and towed to land by a small steamer. The sick are not embarked on these barges, but are landed separately in a special boat. This latter ceremony over, the men were drawn up in batches of one hundred on either side of the main deck, and formally handed over by Ivanoff to the Governor of the prison.

It was a strange sight, although, notwithstanding the dramatic surroundings and incessant clank of chains, one could scarcely describe it as a sad one. There were some haggard faces, of course, chiefly among the young or very aged men, but the majority affected, even if they did not feel, a callous indifference to their surroundings that surprised me. Some even laughed and joked with Ivanoff as he moved in and out of the ranks, comparing identification papers, and restoring money that had been left in his charge. There seemed to be few restrictions with regard to personal property. All had large bundles, and nearly every man a tea-kettle, while many carried boxes of cigarettes and packets of tobacco. One aged reprobate (who had already been here twice) had provided himself with a large palm fan, evidently purchased during the voyage, at Singapore or Colombo. I had for some time been watching the busy scene from the upper deck, when a telegram was handed to Ivanoff, which he rapidly read, and handed to the prison official at his side. A short consultation ensued, after which a name was called out, and answered to by an old man of venerable aspect, who had, up till now, worn a very dejected air, and kept aloof from his companions. Amid breathless silence the message was then read aloud, and I was not surprised, at its conclusion, to see the poor old fellow fall upon the deck, clasp Ivanoff round the knees, and burst into tears, for the telegram was from St. Petersburg to announce that he had been granted a free pardon. It says much for human nature that throughout that crowd of villainous faces there was scarcely one that did not express satisfaction and even pleasure at the news, which was received by a ringing cheer that no one attempted to suppress, but which even some of the guards, who were standing by, joined in. The most hardened cynic could scarcely have stood by unmoved at the scene that followed, when, as they went over the side, every member of his gang shook hands with their old comrade, who in his excitement had flung aside his bundle and kettle, and now stood bare-headed at the gangway. As the barge was slowly moving off, I saw the old fellow secure with nervous, trembling fingers a few kopeks, his worldly wealth, in a piece of dirty paper, which was thrown after and caught by a dozen eager hands. "Prashtchai Brate,"* he said, "this is for good luck," and as the cry came faintly back over the water, "Farewell; good luck at home!" a flood of tears overcame him, and he was led away sobbing like a child to pleasanter quarters by Ivanoff.

Lepsky was shortly afterwards sent ashore, alone in the tug-boat. He looked pale and tired, and cast an eager glance upward, evidently expecting to catch sight of Olga, who had up till now been standing beside me, but she, poor child, had already left the deck, evidently unable to bear the sight. The medical student had thrown the coarse gray cloak over his shoulders with a certain grace, and wore the hideous, shapeless cap slightly on one side, with an attempt at smartness generally assumed by political convicts to distinguish them from the common herd. But the ordeal was a trying one,

---

* "Good-bye, brothers."

and the poor fellow showed evident signs of shame and uneasiness, till permitted to descend the gangway ladder, which he did as quickly as his heavy irons would permit.

Alexandrovsky-Post is a pretty town, considerably larger than Korsakovsky, situated on a plateau surrounded by an amphitheatre of rugged snow-capped hills. A tramway worked by convicts connects it with the landing-place, one-half mile distant, where a long, substantially-built wooden pier and a huge wooden shed for the reception of prisoners are the principal features. Prisoners are confined here for a few hours only, until all are landed. They are then marched under escort to the town, where, as at Korsakovsky, the huge prison stands out in grim relief against the smaller buildings. The latter are chiefly of wood, but very neatly constructed, while the streets are broad and well laid out, with good wooden pavements. The Governor's house, the church, and perhaps a dozen houses of officials are of whitewashed wood, and have gaily-coloured roofs of red or green, which

GOING TO WORK. ALEXANDROVSKY-POST.

relieves to a great extent the depressing aspect of unpainted timber.

It was at one of these that I was welcomed by Mr. Taskine, the Governor of the prison, and his charming wife, the morning following our

ALEXANDROVSKY-POST, SHOWING, ON THE RIGHT, MR. TASKINE'S HOUSE.

arrival. The day was so bright and warm that *déjeuner* had been laid in the verandah, and I was introduced for the first time to a native delicacy known as "Trepang" or sea-slug, which, however, did not inspire me with any desire to renew its acquaintance. It seemed strange to be idling over coffee and cigarettes in the glorious sunshine, under an Italian sky, in a spot which a few short weeks hence would present a picture of Arctic desolation; stranger still, that roses, heliotrope, and other summer flowers should bloom as freely and smell as sweet as in some carefully-tended garden around Paris. I had lately read that the vicinity of Dui (three miles distant) was absolutely sterile, and was therefore the more agreeably surprised.*

There are two prisons at Alexandrovsky-Post,† divided one from the other by a narrow lane a few feet wide. The first and largest contains convicts approaching their time of release and men of good conduct; the second being reserved for the most dangerous class, or those who have committed crime on the island. It would be superfluous to wade through a detailed description of these buildings, which are precisely similar

---

* "Agriculture and gardening are impossible in the vicinity of Dui." (From "Russian and French Prisons." Prince Krapotkine. Ward & Downey, London.)

† See Appendix B.

to those at Korsakovsky-Post, a succession of iron-roofed log huts surrounded by a wooden palisade nearly twenty feet high, nor shall I inflict other dry prison details on the reader, merely remarking that the "Kameras," hospital, and general arrangements were in every respect equal to those at the Southern Settlement.

The two prisons, on the day of my visit, conjointly contained 1,056 men, about a third of whom were confined in the smaller building. The air of sullen severity about the latter contrasted very strongly with the neighbouring building, which presented the usual open and unguarded appearance common to Siberian jails. I noticed, however, that even here a rigid discipline prevailed that, accustomed as I am to the free-and-easy ways of Russian jailers, considerably astonished me. Every warder sprang to attention on being addressed by Taskine. Smoking was strictly forbidden in the "Kameras," and when we passed a prisoner he instantly turned his face to the wall. On the other hand, the "Kameras" were all left open during the day, and the inmates could move about as freely as they pleased in the yard, which measures about forty yards square. It was almost deserted, most of the men being out at work; for, with the exception of tailoring and shoemaking, no labour is carried on within prison walls. Most of the "Kameras" in this building are constructed to contain from fifty to eighty men, and a smaller building in a corner of the yard attracted my attention. I learned that it had formerly been used for the punishment of refractory characters, but was now occupied by a solitary inmate—a tall, brawny-looking ruffian, described by Taskine as the "flogger" of the prison. The post is apparently no sinecure, for this man (himself a convict) dared not venture abroad without protection, and had he passed the night in a "Kamera," would probably have been torn in pieces. The implements of his trade were scattered about the cell, and he seemed to take pleasure in describing their uses; the "Rosgi" or birch, "Kabyla" or "Mare," a bench about two feet high, to which the culprit is strapped face downward, and the dreaded "plet," which can be so wielded as to kill a man with six strokes. The one shown me, and which figures in the accompanying illustration,

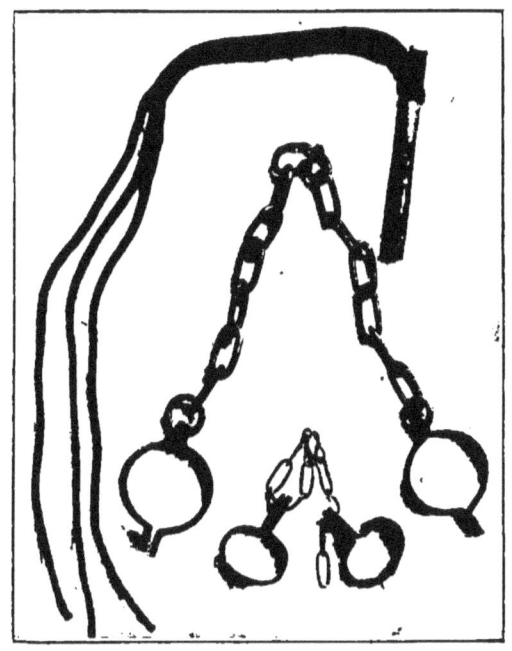

THE "PLET" AND MANACLES AS NOW USED ON SAKHALIN.

was a truly ghastly weapon. It weighed eight pounds, and was attached to a circular handle a foot long and seven inches in circumference. The lash was of solid leather, two and a half feet long, tapering from the handle to three circular thongs the size of a little finger. As many as ninety-nine blows *below the waist* may be given. They are administered from left to right, and *vice versâ*, laying the flesh open in all directions. Death sometimes follows this terrible punishment, which is only administered as a substitute for the death penalty. The "Rosgi," an instrument closely resembling an Eton birch, is generally used, and this may be ordered by the Jail-Governor, but the use of the "plet" can only be sanctioned by the Governor of the District, who, even in murder cases, rarely uses his prerogative.

Taking leave of this objectionable individual and his gruesome relics, we left the yard and proceeded to visit the smaller building, the gateway of which should assuredly have borne Dante's famous inscription. Its dilapidated exterior was only surpassed by the melancholy aspect of the dreary yard, where the incessant clink of fetters fell upon the ear, caused by the aimless wandering to and fro of a number of

FIXING FETTERS, ALEXANDROVSKY-POST, SAKHALIN.

haggard, sinister-looking wretches, the contemplation of whose abject condition seemed to draw a dark veil of human misery over the place, and completely shut out the sunshine and blue sky. A collection of gray-clad corpses could not have presented a more pitiable or lifeless appearance than the unhappy beings who slowly crawled around us, trailing their heavy fettered limbs over the sun-baked ground, and occasionally raising their downcast eyes to steal a furtive look at the sentry, armed with cutlass and revolver, who stood in their midst. Even the knowledge that any one of these men, with object, time, or opportunity, would have slit my throat from ear to ear without a moment's compunction, did not suppress a feeling of compassion that we must occasionally feel for even the most worthless and debased of our fellow-creatures.

The "Kameras" here, unlike those of the neighbouring building, were closely secured, and our entry into one entailed the removal of numerous and complicated bolts and bars, the inmates only being permitted to take exercise in batches of twenty. One can scarcely say that the cells are over-crowded, although the gloom and close, polluted air compared very unfavourably with the light, airy wards that I had previously visited. The inmates, without a single exception, wore leg-chains, and two or three were also handcuffed. I found that two of the latter had committed a violent assault on a warder, and that the third had nearly succeeded in escaping from the island. One of the "Kameras" we entered contained eight men chained to wheelbarrows, a punishment dreaded as much as, if not more than, a flogging with the "plet," but which, like the latter, is only applied in cases where less violent measures have entirely failed. The punishment, severe as it is, could be made much more so, for the barrow is, though heavy, little larger than a toy, the chain on which it is secured being of light steel links, and eight feet long, which admits of the barrow being propped up at night against the sleeping platforms. Taskine told me that this penalty can be inflicted for three years at a stretch, but that six months is its

CONVICT CHAINED TO WHEELBARROW.

usual limit, and even this seemed to me to be not only excessive but barbarous. It is, however, my object to expose the dark as well as the light side of this Russian Exile System, although it is only fair to add that, in the opinion of most Russian prison officials I have met, this inhuman practice should be abolished without delay. Sakhalin is now the only place throughout Siberia where it is enforced.

The punishment cells of this prison proved full of interest, for they contained not only the notorious convict Pashchenko, who had escaped under very sensational circumstances a few years before, but also two of the chief actors in the Onor tragedy, which excited so much indignation in England, and which, indeed, had been the primary cause of this, my third visit to Siberia.* The dark cells are all in one building. There are six of these kennels (for the fact that they measured thirteen feet by eight feet, and were in total darkness, surely justifies the name), and the first we entered was occupied by Pashchenko, a tall, refined-looking man about forty years old, with steely-blue eyes and a long, fair beard, who seemed dazed and bewildered when, simul-

* See Appendix C.

taneously with a brilliant flood of sunshine, we entered his tiny cell. The convict wore tweed, and the cleanliness of his linen was remarkable. I note these details in connection with what followed.

It appeared from Taskine's account that Pashchenko had originally been transported (for forgery) to Sakhalin, but had escaped a few years after, by the aid of a friendly whaler, to San Francisco. Here he had lived for two or three years, and by dint of sheer hard work had established a lucrative business in the private inquiry line. Business of vital importance one day necessitating his presence at Vladivostok, he resolved to run all risks and embark for the Siberian port; for very large interests were involved, and, money being of no object, he had no doubt of being able, in case of trouble, to silence the police. Provided, therefore, with a clever disguise, he landed at Vladivostok, only to be instantly rearrested (through the treachery of a friend in America) and sent back to Sakhalin. He was here to be tried on the charge of murdering a native Gilyak, who had tried to impede his escape. I then inquired of Taskine how long he had been here, and was told three years. "Three months, you mean," I replied incredulously. "No, three years," said Taskine decidedly, and the poor manacled wretch nodded silently as if to endorse this outrageous statement. "He is awaiting trial by a military tribunal," added Taskine, "for the case is an exceptionally bad one." I knew that if found guilty this meant death, and my blood boiled at the inhumanity that had kept this man languishing in a dark den for so many weary months. I was silent, however, for it would have availed nothing to speak, nor would it have lightened Pashchenko's lot. It would, moreover, have mortally offended my host, who, I have reason to know, is both humane and considerate. But habitual contact with criminals will harden the most gentle nature, and I have no doubt that Taskine saw nothing to pity in the lot of this unhappy being, whose sufferings must have equalled, if they did not surpass, the tortures of those immured in the famous "Oubliettes" of the Bastille.

Two adjoining cells were occupied by the other convicts, Vassilief and Kalenik, who presented a pitiable and degrading spectacle. The terrible experience undergone by Vassilief had deprived him of his reason a few days before, and he sat crouching in a corner of his cell crooning softly to himself, and apparently quite unconscious of our presence. His companion, Kalenik, a short, wiry-looking little fellow, with a bright, intelligent face, greeted us with a smile and a request for more tobacco, which was immediately sent for. His unconcerned, almost cheerful manner was the more remarkable in that he was in a few days to receive ninety-nine lashes from the "plet," which were fated to result in his death. Vassilief had also been sentenced to the same punishment, but was eventually spared on account of his mental condition.

It was a relief to emerge from this abode of crime and insanity, and to drive away through the pleasant sunshine to the workshops, half a mile distant. These consist of half-a-dozen lofty wooden sheds with corrugated iron roofs, where work of various kinds was going on under the superintendence of armed sentries. Perhaps a third of the men employed were in ordinary dress, having completed their term in prison, and were now living in snug cottages in and about Alexandrovsky-Post. Every shed is used for a particular trade, the first we entered containing four forges. Here agricultural implements, such as ploughs, harrows, spades, were being turned out in large numbers, a great part of the material used being stripped from the hull of a Norwegian steamer wrecked here two years ago. Shoeing is also carried on here, for the prison stables contained more than thirty horses for farm work. Adjoining this was a building for iron moulding. The engine of the steam launch that brought us ashore was made here, and I was shown some very creditable specimens in the shape of locks, and even rifles and revolvers. A steam saw, hard by, worked by an engine by Ransome & Co., of Chelsea, was turning out over a hundred planks a day.

I here made the acquaintance of a noted character, one Sokoloff, a fine-looking old man over eighty-four years of age, who had passed over fifty years of his life in penal servitude, and had escaped no less than eight times from various Russian prisons. Sokoloff had twice been flogged with the "plet," a fact he lost no opportunity of proudly relating to strangers. Some dozen lighters, lying in the little river Alexandrovna, and a large boiler, with which it is proposed to furnish the town with electric light, were also in course of construction, but I think I have already said enough, without mentioning other penal industries, to show that there is, at any rate, no lack of labour at Sakhalin, and that the demoralising influence of enforced idleness is, although unfortunately common enough in Siberia, quite unknown on the island. I should add that the freed workmen are paid by the Government at the rate of so much per day.

I was to leave next day for the settlements in the interior of the island, but was glad, before doing so, to accept Madame Taskine's proposition to accompany her to the prison schools and orphanage, of which she has the control and supervision. A short and pleasant walk through shady woods and grassy meadows plentifully sprinkled with the pretty white lily known as "Oreilles d'Ours," brought us to the building, which has only lately been completed. This institution is exclusively for the children of prisoners, of whom there were forty-eight of both sexes, the age of admittance being from three to fourteen years. We arrived during play hours, and, the matron being absent, a rosy-cheeked little girl in the school dress of brown serge, snowy apron, and light-blue hood, took us round the place, pointed out the school-room, playground, and dormitories with pride, and smiled with pleasure when I remarked on the neatness and cleanliness that everywhere met the eye. There is a farm attached to the place, and the ground round the building was apportioned out in miniature gardens. The boys are taught a trade, and, as soon as they are old enough, earn a livelihood, while the girls are

GROUP OF CONVICTS, ALEXANDROVSKY-POST.

brought up as domestic servants. Both sexes also receive a sound, practical education. This admirably-conducted institution is chiefly supported by voluntary contributions, and is only partly subsidised by Government, and this, Madame Taskine informed me, was to be Olga Elnikoff's future home, although every effort had been made to induce her to reconsider her decision, and, for her mother's sake, to return in the *Yaroslav* to Russia. This, however, she utterly declined to do, or in any way to alter her original programme. The marriage with Lepsky had therefore been arranged to take place on the morrow. Olga had meanwhile remained on board the ship, but would, at the conclusion of the ceremony, enter at once upon her duties at the orphanage.

I had occasion, before starting, to return to the *Yaroslav* for the pelisse and revolver that constituted my only luggage. The captain and officers, with the exception of Ivanoff, were ashore, and the decks and ward-room presented a silent, deserted appearance. Olga Elnikoff was lying in a long deck-chair near the companion stairway. The poor child was fast asleep, and looked so worn and in need of rest that I dared not awaken her. A book lay open on her lap—a tiny volume that I had given her a few days before, chiefly because the plot and incidents of the pathetic little story it contained so closely coincided, in many ways, with her own sad, restless life. The very phrase she had just been reading might, under the circumstances, have been written by herself, for the letter in which it occurs is headed "A Russian Prison." "The prison walls vanish," it ran, "and I see the great elms and the flat meadows and the thatched cottages all sleeping in the English sunlight. I hear the voices of the English children singing 'He hath brought light to them that sit in darkness, and in the shadow of death, and I dream that there is a God who smiles, at least, upon England.'"*

I never saw her again.

---

* "Mlle. Ixe," by Lanoe Falconer, Pseudonym Library, London.

CHAPTER VI.

A JOURNEY IN THE INTERIOR.

WE galloped out of the town about three o'clock in a springless but not uncomfortable country cart, procured by Taskine, who, although I expected to return within three days, had fitted me out with provisions for as many weeks. He had also provided me with an escort in the shape of a huge Cossack (Ivan by name), who bristled with knives and revolvers, and looked like accounting for half-a-dozen armed bandits at least. The distance to Rykovskaya is nearly fifty English miles, and, as part of our road lay through dark, dense forests, said to be infested with runaway convicts, I was glad enough of his company.

A mile or so from the town we passed the cemetery, where a young Englishman, found drowned on the beach, had been interred a few days previously. Little was known about the circumstances leading to his death, excepting that he had endeavoured to cross from the mainland in an open boat which a sudden squall had capsized, drowning all the occupants but one native, who swam ashore, and brought news of the disaster. I photographed the spot (thinking that fate might some day bring me across the poor fellow's friends in England), and was afterwards glad that I had done so.

Shortly after this we left the highway to follow the sea-beach, which, the tide having receded for a long distance, rattled like asphalte under our horses' feet, and enabled us to cover seven odd miles in less than half an hour. We then rejoined the high-road leading direct to our destination. Turning inland we came, on the fringe of the forest, upon a native village, where some Gilyaks were drying fish for winter consumption, and mending their bows and arrows. The oily stench of their ramshackle, smoke-blackened huts and filthy rags was noticeable for many yards, and their repulsive, mask-like faces leered out at us like evil spirits as we drove past. The encampment was surrounded by dogs of a much larger and fiercer breed than those at Por-na-maré, who snarled and growled viciously, and would probably, if loose, have attacked us.

The native population of Sakhalin is rapidly dying out, and it is probable that they do not now number more than five thousand souls in all. These consist of Gilyaks in the north and Ainus in the southern part of the island. The latter are indigenous to Yezo, and were driven by Japanese oppression to cross the Straits of La Perouse and seek refuge on the neighbouring island. They differ from other Mongolian races by their luxuriant growth of hair and beard, the entire body sometimes presenting a hirsute appearance. The Ainus also possess other attributes, so interesting that they have been named by ethnological students "the Aztecs of the North."

The Gilyak characteristics, on the other hand,

may be summed up in three words: dirt, drink, and disease, the two latter having been greatly augmented since their intercourse with Europeans. There are few races, save perhaps in the remoter parts of Polynesia or the African continent, that present so low a condition. The Gilyak is of tawny complexion, and wears his coarse black hair tied up, Chinese fashion, in a short pigtail. He is short in stature, barely attaining five feet in height, but is thick-set and muscular, and well fitted for the life he leads of hardship and exposure. His summer garb is a thin, almost transparent garment, made of fish-skin and quite waterproof; while in winter he is clad in coarse skins, generally of the dog, wolf, or fox. The Gilyak is naturally of an indolent disposition, and, like his dogs, subsists entirely on fish. Some are skilful at trapping, and the use of the bow and arrow, which enables them to earn a little by the sale of skins; but the majority prefer to live an idle, aimless existence throughout the warm season, as soon as they have collected enough food for sustenance

BEARDED AINU AND GILYAKS, SAKHALIN.

throughout the long, dreary winter. It has been said that many of the Gilyaks subsist on rewards offered by the Government for the capture of escaped convicts, but this is a gross exaggeration. Not only is the Gilyak far too lazy to willingly undertake such an arduous task, but the small reward of three roubles for every restored runaway is scarcely sufficient to tempt even a savage to endanger his personal safety. Should, therefore, a " white sable " * cross his path, the Gilyak generally (to use an American expression) " has business elsewhere," and the convict pursues his way unmolested.

Leaving the native village and its unsavoury occupants, we travelled on till sunset through a country of dense forests alternating with stretches of pasture land. As we advanced inland the temperature fell, and on the hills signs of winter were still visible in the shape of snow a few inches deep by the roadside. In the valleys, however, this had completely disappeared, for

---

* A Gilyak nickname for escaped convicts.

the bright, brief summer had resumed its reign. The sward was carpeted with fragrant wild flowers, while on every side field and forest presented an ever-changing kaleidoscope of colour, varying from darkest russet to the tenderest shades of green. Some snowy peaks glittering on the horizon, and the still sunlit meadows, tinkle of cattle bells, and scent of freshly mown hay, recalled idle summer days in Switzerland, and so glorious was the scenery and pleasant the day that I almost regretted its termination, when, at dusk, we reached the first station, Arkovo. When we resumed our journey night had fallen, and a thin crescent moon was rising in a sky powdered with stars.

It now became too cold for comfort, and the crisp night air penetrated even my heavy reindeer pelisse. I had (at Ivan's suggestion) loaded my revolver at Arkovo, and now kept it handy in case of attack, for unarmed wayfarers have been robbed, and even murdered, here. Night travel in Sakhalin is decidedly trying, even to a person of average strength of nerve, which I hope I may claim to be, and I must own to a feeling of relief when this part of the drive was over. Out in the open it was all plain sailing; but the lights and shadows of a pine forest in bright starlight are especially disquieting when the traveller is momentarily expecting a blow on the back of the head with an axe or bludgeon. I could have sworn twenty times to the presence of human figures by the roadside, and even Ivan's experienced eye was deceived more than once. One portion of the forest we came to presented a curious and picturesque appearance. It seemed as though the woods were illuminated on either side, from the roadside to their innermost depths, with thousands of coloured lamps. The illusion was caused by some peasants from a neighbouring village, who had during the day been opening a clearing, for agricultural purposes, by the usual Siberian method, viz., burning through the lower trunk of the tree. The flames had then gradually subsided, leaving myriads of glowing sparks behind them.

Towards ten o'clock we drove through Derbynskaya, a pretty village situated on the river Tym—a shallow, insignificant stream, but one of the two principal rivers of the island, which is very badly watered. Here we changed horses, and an hour later reached our destination, Rykovskaya, a place of considerable size, which reminded me of a Christmas card, with its starlit church, quiet main street, and prim white dwellings, with lights gleaming through their red-curtained windows. M. Boutakoff, the Natchalnik (Commandant), a fine-looking, soldierly man about fifty, in gray and yellow uniform, received me with true Russian hospitality at the gate of the garden fronting his house, and ushered me into a room full of ladies in evening dress, and blazing with light, a somewhat trying ordeal for a dusty, travel-stained man with no luggage. Two of the young ladies were, I found, daughters of M. Boutakoff, who was a widower. The third was Mdlle. Ovtchinikoff, a tall, fair-haired girl from Derbynskaya, quite pretty enough to create a sensation in a London or Paris drawing-room. I have experienced many surprises in Siberia, both agreeable and otherwise, but the supper that followed my arrival here savoured of dreamland. Any anticipations I may have formed of the interior of Sakhalin certainly did not comprise pretty women, smart frocks, the French language in perfection, and a grand piano, upon which Mdlle. Boutakoff was as proficient as most amateurs. Time passed so quickly and agreeably that every one was surprised when five o'clock chimed from the church hard by. We then separated, the Natchalnik showing me to a tiny, well-furnished bedroom, where the dawn was already struggling through the chintz window-curtains. And I fell asleep dreaming that I was really awake in Paris, and that my evening at Rykovskaya was nothing more than an empty, feverish dream.

Part II.

THERE are three penal establishments in the interior of Sakhalin, of which Rykovskaya, built in 1879, is the oldest. It may seem a paradox (but it is no less a fact) when I say that these island prisons are not, in the true sense of the word, prisons at all. They are simply huge barracks, open to the world and innocent of bolts and bars. The one at Derbynskaya, for instance, was not even surrounded by the usual palisade; while Rykovskaya consists of half-a-dozen barnlike buildings, only one of which is actually used as a place of confinement for local evildoers. The remainder of the exiles are free, so long as they are well-behaved, to roam about the village for a radius of three miles around it. A very small minority wear prison dress, and perhaps a dozen of those in the cells wore chains. Rykovskaya prison only resembles a jail in that it has a good school, a clean, well-managed infirmary, and a large well-stocked farm attached to the establishment, on which convicts are compelled to work (in summer) eight hours a day. The rest of their time is at their own disposal; in fact, they cannot be described as prisoners at all, but "settlers," many of them living in their own dwellings, and outside the prison altogether.

Baths are unknown in most Siberian establishments. I was awakened about nine o'clock by a bearded giant in a crimson kaftan, who with great deliberation placed a small iron washstand in the middle of the room, and having presented me with a piece of soap, took up a position, towel in hand, beside it, from which he utterly declined to stir. It was, apparently, this domestic's duty to pour a thin trickling stream of water over the hands and wash them clear of soap. This ceremony completed, he patiently waited until I had restored the towel, and slowly vanished, taking the washstand with him. This completed my ablutions for the day, and as dressing operations were equally brief, I was soon ready to accompany my host on his daily round of inspection.

The (so-called) Rykovskaya jail is best described as a collection of old, but not uncleanly, wooden huts, open to the world. I use the term advisedly, for there is no outer wall, bolt, or padlock visible. The huts, each one containing two "Kameras," are four in number, and as the unbarred windows of the latter look on to the public roadway, it would be anomalous to dignify this insecure building by the name of prison. As I have said before, "barracks" is a far more suitable term for this free-and-easy, open-air penitentiary. There is nothing about the place suggestive of penal life. The inmates for the most part wear the high boots, black velvet breeches, and scarlet "Kaftan" of the peasantry. Not a jailer is to be seen, though a knot of so-called prisoners are chatting by the open gateway as contentedly as any group of English yokels. It is the hour for dinner (always served within the prison walls), and in another twenty minutes or so every one will resume work in the fields, unaccompanied by escort of any kind.

The "Kameras" here closely resemble those

at the coast settlements, with one or two trifling exceptions. The "nares" or sleeping platforms, for instance, were (unlike any I had previously seen) divided into bunks by wooden partitions, while each man was provided with a stout blanket in addition to his mattress and pillow. One ward was set apart for aged and crippled convicts, and another for youngsters of sixteen to twenty years old, who are thus effectually separated from the more hardened criminals. Most of the convicts were employed on the prison farm, which covers many hundred acres of ground, and perhaps a third were told off for work in the gardens, which were well stocked, and supplied not only Derbynskaya, but also Alexandrovsky-Post, with vegetables. A saw-mill and some brick-works about a mile away constituted the sole mechanical labour.

There is a good school here for the children of convicts, which, though not so complete in its internal arrangements as the one at Alexandrovsky-Post, was clean and well managed. It contained eighty-five boys and thirty-two girls, under the care of a political exile and his wife, who was voluntarily sharing his captivity. The school-room bore evident signs of work in the shape of well-filled bookcases, maps, and a globe, while in an adjoining apartment were two or three sewing-machines, several looms, and a lathe.

The hospital at Rykovskaya was even superior to those on the coast. It consists of three neat wooden buildings, one for men, one for women, and the third, some distance away, for infectious cases. The first ward I visited contained twenty-two patients. Each patient occupied a comfortable iron bedstead, at the foot of which was a blackboard showing the nature of his complaint. A gray felt carpet was laid between the beds the length of the room, which was bright, clean, and airy. Dr. Tropine, of the Military Medical Academy of St. Petersburg, was in charge of this establishment, and told me that though pulmonary and rheumatic complaints are frequent, epidemics of any severity are unknown throughout the island. The infectious ward contained only three cases: a woman and her two children, who were suffering from scarlet fever of a mild type. I was surprised to find that, in addition to most of the modern surgical appliances, the pharmacy contained several patent medicines, some of them English. But Dr. Tropine is an enthusiast in his profession, and the Rykovskaya Hospital is acknowledged to be the best conducted establishment of the kind in Sakhalin—one might almost add throughout Eastern Siberia.

Having visited the farm buildings, stables, and storehouses, we walked down the main street of the village and knocked at the door of a cottage at its extreme end. We were at once admitted by a neatly-dressed little woman, who is undoubtedly the most interesting criminal convict at present on Sakhalin. This is Sophie Bloeffstein, whose career was the talk of Europe a few years ago, and whose gigantic and successful frauds have earned her the sobriquet of "Zolotaya Routchka," or the "Golden Hand." How this clever little lady began life is not quite

K

clear, although she is well known, not only to the Russian, but also to the Paris and Vienna police, having upon one occasion (in her temporary character of Queen of the Demi-Monde) spent over £40,000, the money of her dupes, in one year in the Austrian capital. Books have been written and songs published throughout Russia about the "Golden Hand," who now, having completed her long term of imprisonment, lives quietly on the outskirts of Rykovskaya, and supplies the village with eggs and vegetables. Sophie shook my hand warmly, but not that of the "Natchalnik." It would not have been etiquette although they appeared to be on excellent terms. We all three then sat down and partook of some delicious iced "kvas," while our hostess very willingly related some of the most striking incidents of her eventful life in fluent French and German. She is a small, slightly-built woman, with sharp, clearly-cut features and light-blue eyes, and still shows traces of beauty that even prison life has failed to entirely obliterate.

That the "Golden Hand's" past life had not been altogether peaceful was evident, for

SOPHIE BLOEFFSTEIN, "THE GOLDEN HAND."

deep scars showed that the ear-rings had been torn through her left ear no less than three times. Sophie was dressed in a black skirt and a loose mauve *peignoir*, her hair being fringed across with some attempt at coquetry. We talked of London and Paris, and she admitted that she preferred the latter. "London was so *triste*; almost as bad as Sakhalin! Paris and Vienna were very different," added the "Golden Hand," who I have since heard managed to worm her way into good society in the former city until detected by Russian police agents. But Sophie's greatest *coup* was when she first achieved renown by pressing her attentions on the Shah of Persia, when the latter visited St. Petersburg, for the purpose of relieving him, if possible, of some of his diamonds. She even succeeded in having her private car attached to His Majesty's special train, but was foiled at the last moment and sent for a long term of imprisonment to Eastern Siberia. Here, having regained her provisional liberty, she organised a band of robbers and cut-throats whose services she controlled long after their terms had expired. She was then relegated to the prison of Alexandrovsky-Post, but managed to escape on two occasions, and once nearly

THE "GOLDEN HAND" AFTER HER FIRST ESCAPE AND RE-CAPTURE. SAKHALIN.

got clear of the island. I doubted (and so, I think, did the "Natchalnik") her assurance that she never would attempt to escape again, but now intended to end her days in peace at Rykovskaya. "I have had my day," she said, with a pleasant smile, as we took our leave, and it is to be hoped that, if even unconsciously, she spoke the truth.

Although I examined it closely on the way back to Alexandrovsky-Post, it will be unnecessary to describe the prison of Derbynskaya, for the simple reason that it is, although rather smaller, precisely similar in every other respect to the Rykovskaya establishment. Suffice it to say that, if I was agreeably surprised by the prisons on the coast, I was infinitely more so by those in the interior, and I left for the silver mines of Eastern Siberia more than ever convinced of a fact obviously apparent to any one who has studied the Siberian exile system seriously and without bias, namely, that the object of the Government is not so much to punish crime as to colonise Russian Asia.

Time would not admit of a visit to Onor,* for, although only forty versts distant, the road was in such an unfinished state that it would have necessitated a journey of at least a week, by which time the *Yaroslav* would have sailed away, leaving me without opportunity of reaching the mainland for an indefinite period. Moreover, the chief actors in the alleged tragedy at Onor were now in Rykovskaya, so that it would have been useless to proceed to the former place. I made the acquaintance, among others, of Khanoff, who impressed me very favourably, although it is not always fair to judge by appearances. The "Natchalnik" had upheld him throughout, and, even now, refused to believe in his guilt. However this may be, my independent inquiries among the villagers proved, at any rate, that things were grossly exaggerated, and the reported convoys of corpses could scarcely have escaped the notice of the young ladies of Boutakoff's household, who were at first amused and then

---

* See Appendix C.

highly indignant at the accounts that had appeared in the English newspapers. "What will they say next in England?" lisped pretty Mdlle. Ovtchinikoff. "That we walk about in the streets arm-in-arm with the bears?"

Alexandrovsky-Post was safely reached on the fourth day from departure, after a pleasant journey, unmarred by accident or wet weather. I found my friend Taskine in a state of great excitement, for theatricals* were to be performed by some freed exiles the next evening, and he had consented to act as stage-manager. But I was unfortunately unable to attend this unique performance, for daybreak on the following morning found the *Yaroslav* cleaving her way to Vladivostok through the cold blue waters of the Gulf of Tartary.

---

* See Appendix D.

CHAPTER VII.

VLADIVOSTOK * AND THE SIBERIAN RAILWAY.

I AM not generally fastidious. A long course of Chinese and Siberian travel, to say nothing of various wanderings in other strange lands, has more or less inured me to discomfort and hardship, and, although I strongly object to doing so, I can on occasion "rough it" with the best. But the "Hôtel de la Corne d'Or" at Vladivostok was, even to my practised eye, a horrible revelation. The phenomenal filth of the place beggared description. I can only portray the accommodation as a collection of pigsties, of which a drinking-bar (also used as a *salle-à-manger*) formed the unsavoury nucleus.

---

* A name signifying in the Russian language, "Dominion of the East."

Finding on inquiry that one of the aforesaid pigsties was to let for the modest sum of ten roubles per night, I followed a barefooted scorbutic youth in filthy shirt-sleeves, and proceeded to inspect a dark, kennel-like den that a dog would have turned from in disgust. The rotten flooring, riddled with rat-holes, looked scarcely strong enough to support even the rickety table and rusty iron bedstead that, with its ragged, discoloured counterpane, lurked in the gloom of a far corner. Long strips of mildewed paper, detached by age and damp from the grimy walls, waved idly to and fro in the breeze that, entering through a broken window, brought with it an overpowering stench from a cesspool immediately beneath. To sleep in such a place was out of the question, and having nothing of importance to detain me in Vladivostok, I resolved to start that night for Khabarovsk.

Like most Siberian cities, Vladivostok looks its best at a distance. Although there are several fine buildings, comprising the Governor's

Palace and Naval Club, the greater portion of the town presents the untidy, unfinished appearance peculiar to Siberian cities. Even the principal street is a dreary, straggling thoroughfare, unpaved, and ankle-deep in dust or mud, as the case may be. An attempt had been made at a public garden, but the trees are stunted, withered-looking things, and the flowers conspicuous by their absence. The sylvan illusion is kept up, however, by a mangy-looking grass-plot and painted wooden kiosk, where a regimental band performs twice a week throughout the summer.

At first sight, Vladivostok is imposing enough, with its frowning earthworks, huge barracks, and bustling wharves and warehouses. From dawn to sunset the low green hills around the harbour swarm with white-clad soldiers at work on the fortifications. Snake-like torpedo-boats glide noiselessly in all directions, and wicked-looking guns of modern and deadly type peer out of the most unlikely places, for defensive precautions are being carried on with a restless persistence that must eventually crown Vladivostok Queen of Fortresses in the Far East. There does not exist a finer harbour for strategical purposes in the world, and the combined fleets of France and Russia could ride at ease on its blue, land-locked surface. But it is ice-bound during nearly five months of the year, although the fact that, at a distance of only ten miles from the coast, there is open water all the year round, must be extremely galling to the Muscovite mind. Efforts have been made to keep a passage open throughout the winter for warships by means of ice-boats, but, hitherto, with poor results.

The population of Vladivostok consists of about 30,000 Russians, Chinese, and Koreans. The trade of the place is chiefly in German hands, the better class of Russians being nearly all officials and naval and military officers, for, in addition to its importance as a military centre, Vladivostok is also the headquarters of the Russian Pacific Squadron. This, in summer, conduces greatly to the animation of the place.

Dances and dinner parties follow each other in rapid succession, the theatre is generally occupied by a theatrical company, the Naval Club crowded nightly, and the round of gaiety, not to say dissipation, is kept up with unflagging spirit till early October, when shortening days and cold gray fogs herald the season when, a few weeks later, the sunlit harbour and smiling hills shall be converted by the iron grip of winter into a desolate waste of ice and snow.

A glance at the map will show that my route from Vladivostok was, theoretically, simple enough. My first objective point was the village of Boussè, at the head of the Oussouri River, whence a river steamer runs to Khabarovsk (a large city, and the seat of the Governor-General of Eastern Siberia), situated at the junction of the Oussouri and Amour Rivers. I found that the Siberian Railway was already in working order, and would take me to Tchernigovka, a small village about 130 miles away. From this point I must complete the remaining 150 odd miles to Boussè, in a "Telega," or country cart.

The one train of the day was to leave at midnight, so, entrusting my bag to a railway official, I returned about sundown to the hotel in quest of refreshment. A meal (pleasantly described as dinner by the proprietor) was in progress, at which I was agreeably surprised to find myself seated next to an old acquaintance. Mr. K—— (whom I had met a few months previously in St. Petersburg) was a Russian engineer, employed in the eastern section of the railway, and was to-night returning to his station, Nova-Silya, situated about half-way to Boussè. We therefore agreed to travel together to Tchernigovka, the present terminus of the line, although my friend strongly advised me to postpone my departure and travel to Khabarovsk by sea, viâ Nikolaefsk, in a small coasting steamer which would be leaving Vladivostok in a few days' time. As this, however, meant a useless detour of about 1,500 miles, the plan hardly suited my views. Notwithstanding, the outlook was black enough. It appeared that the entire tract of country lying north of Tchernigovka had, for some weeks, been inundated by heavy rains, which had overflowed Lake Khanka and submerged the post road, in places, to a depth of several feet. K—— was himself by no means certain of reaching his destination, and under the circumstances, greatly doubted my being able to reach Boussè at all. Even in the event of dry weather, it was extremely improbable that the floods would subside for at least a fortnight, and at present the mails were unable to get either way. As my friend, however, kindly offered me hospitality at Nova-Silya until I was able to proceed on my journey, I determined, after some hesitation, to make the attempt. Anything would be better than a lengthened *séjour* at the "Corne d'Or." We therefore set out for the railway station, a palatial brick building, at eleven o'clock, and joined a well-dressed crowd of both sexes who were partaking of tea and less innocent beverages in the "Restaurant." Some of the ladies wore high evening gowns, a strange mystery cleared up by Mr. K——, who informed me that the departure of the nightly mail was looked upon in Vladivostok society as a fashionable rendezvous. Among those present was Mr. S——, an English merchant residing in Nikolaefsk, who had just returned from an unsuccessful attempt to reach Boussè, and his account of the road beyond Nova-Silya was discouraging enough. The mud, he said, was never below the axles, and he had more than once been obliged to swim for his life. Mr. S—— strongly urged me to accompany him on the *Strelok*, the small steamer I have mentioned, which, it now seemed, would sail in less than a week for Nikolaefsk. But it was too late now to alter my decision, so we adjourned to a small table to drink to my better success in a bottle of well-iced " Pommery." The scene was a gay one, and the brightly-lit room, with its glittering *buffet*, brilliant uniforms, and well-dressed women, astonished me considerably, while the well-appointed station and luxurious waiting-room augured well for the comfort of the journey. But this illusion, alas, was quickly dispelled, when, having secured my ticket (for five roubles), I saw the carriage in which we were to travel. K—— informed me that it was a third-class car. If so, I sincerely pity the impecunious tourist who, in the dim future, attempts the through journey from the Pacific to St. Petersburg. The carriages contained no seats whatever, unless twelve wooden sleeping platforms ranged one above the other across their breadth can be so called. As we numbered over twenty passengers, moving space was somewhat limited; indeed, most of us stood up the whole time, the only alternative being to lie down upon the floor. I reposed, or rather reclined on one of the upper planks between a gentleman in sheepskins and a Chinese platelayer, and had reason for several days to remember my bedfellows. K—— was luckily provided with an extra pillow, which, with my fur pelisse, somewhat softened my hard couch, from which I arose at daybreak, bruised and aching in every limb. A flickering oil lantern, which just made darkness visible, was the only light provided, and when, the night being cold, the air was entirely excluded, the hot, stuffy smell of sheepskins and over-crowded humanity became intolerable. I have read, since my return to England, glowing accounts of the Siberian Railway, but these I cannot honestly endorse, at any rate in the Vladivostok section. I am not speaking of comfort. I know the country far too well ever to expect that in Siberia, and the crowded cattle-pens (for they were little better) caused me little inconvenience. But apart from this, the line is abominably laid. I need say no more than that it took us thirteen hours to cover 130 versts (about the same distance as London to Birmingham), and that this portion of the line is looked upon as permanently fit for traffic.

According to present calculations, the Trans-Siberian Railway, of which the Tsarevitch turned the first sod at Vladivostok in 1891, will be completed in 1901, but many experienced engineers, with whom I came in contact on the works are of the opinion that the entire line will not be in proper working order for at least ten years later. The line will extend from Vladivostok to Irkoutsk (viâ Khabarovsk and across Lake Baikal), and from Irkoutsk (viâ Krasnoyarsk) to Omsk, and thence direct to the main system at Samara. The difficulties are enormous, especially in the Vladivostok section, where dense forests, fever, and clouds of mosquitoes render the work not only arduous, but extremely injurious to health. The other two sections also present serious difficulties, and while those encircling the passage of Lake Baikal are to be temporarily surmounted by steamers in summer, and in winter by ice crushers,* a number of rivers must also be crossed, including the broad, turbulent Yenisei. The latter will probably be negotiated by means of pontoons, although a project is now under consideration for the construction of a permanent bridge of stone and iron. Beyond

---

* Each of these is to cost 800,000 roubles, and is to be constructed so as to cut through ice five feet thick.

this point all is plain sailing, for trains from European Russia are already running to the city of Omsk in Western Siberia, only a few hundred versts away.

The construction of the far Eastern portion of the line has up till lately been greatly hampered by the scarcity of labour. Thinking to remedy this, the Government authorities decided in 1893 to import a number of convicts from Sakhalin. A gang of three thousand were therefore located in charge of a small number of Cossacks in barracks specially built for them on the outskirts of Vladivostok. The scheme worked well, for the men were well paid, and enjoyed almost complete liberty, which, however, was eventually abused. Six months had scarcely elapsed when crime became so frequent that it became unsafe to venture into the streets at night, and the inhabitants of Vladivostok began to realise that thieves and cut-throats are not the most desirable fellow-citizens, especially after dark. Matters came to a crisis when a young French naval officer was robbed and murdered in broad daylight within rifle-shot of the main street. The crime was proved, beyond doubt, to be the work of a convict. An indignation meeting of the townspeople was held, and, within a month, the jail-birds were on the way back to their island prison, and Vladivostok breathed freely once more. The work has since been carried on entirely by soldiers, Koreans, and Chinese.

A steaming glass of fragrant tea at Nikolsk, a large garrison town, early next morning, somewhat revived me after a sleepless night. Nikolsk has at present the largest garrison, Vladivostok excepted, in the littoral province, the troops being located in barracks built some centuries ago by the Chinese. On re-entering the train, it was a relief to find that most of our fellow-passengers had taken their departure. This enabled one, at any rate, to sit down on the hard, unyielding benches, as the train crawled slowly on through the flat, uninteresting country, only relieved at long intervals by a solitary clump of fir-trees, or brown, stagnant pools, rotting in the sunshine. The speed was terribly slow. It reminded me of a certain journey I once made in the Holy Land, where a favourite game among the youth along the line was to jump on and off the steps of the carriages for a mile or two during the passage of the daily trains. At last, towards midday, a protracted shriek from the engine announced that the terminus was in sight, and a few moments later we steamed into the little station of Tchernigovka, a neat but unfinished building of whitewashed timber with a red zinc roof. Here a "Tarantass" was awaiting us, but my friend having business to transact, I took advantage of the delay to try and refresh the inner man. The menu set out by the local Spiers and Pond was scarcely appetising. It consisted of black bread, some dubious butter, half-a-dozen sardines, dried and discoloured by age, a chopped onion floating in a saucer of rancid oil, a piece of smoked salmon, flanked by some dirt-encrusted plates and glasses, and two or three bottles of spirits. These, with some gaudily-coloured advertisements of ales and mineral waters on the wall, dignified the dark little den by the name of "Restaurant." I was faint with hunger, however, which I partially appeased with fish and black bread, for experience has taught me the wisdom, in Siberia, of eating while you may; but I soon regretted this frugal meal, which was speedily followed by a raging and unquenchable thirst.

K—— returned about three o'clock, having taken lunch with his friends, and all being ready, we climbed into the "Tarantass," an old though comfortable vehicle, and jingled through the squalid village and out on to the open sandy plains beyond. The day was bright and warm, the road in good order, and here, at any rate, there were few signs of trouble ahead. We had luckily only just cleared the village when the carriage gave a sudden lurch that nearly deposited me in the road, and brought us to a standstill, which was scarcely surprising, seeing that a hind wheel had come off. K—— sent back our driver for a blacksmith, and coolly lit a cigarette, an example which I soon followed, for in Siberia, as in Turkey, "Hurry is the devil's," and I foresaw a delay of at least a couple of hours. But assistance arrived in less than half the time, and although the smith had evidently looked upon the wine that is red, he quickly repaired the damage, and sent us on our way rejoicing. We reached Prokhori, the first station, twenty-one versts distant, within two hours, and immediately changing horses, were well on our way to Spask, the second, before five o'clock. Our "troika" of rough, wiry little ponies was a good one, and with a merry clashing of bells we dashed along at a rate that made me tremble more than once for the safety of the wheel.

Had it not been for the gnawing, ever-present pain of hunger, the drive would have been more than enjoyable, for our way lay through a lovely country, closely resembling the most picturesque parts of Southern England. The land about here is of the kind that, "tickled with a hoe, laughs with a harvest," and seemed fairly well populated, judging from the snug-looking homesteads, rich pasturage, and broad strips of cultivated land, sprinkled here and there with the bright scarlet "kaftans" of "Moujiks," who are most of them flaxen-haired, blue-eyed emigrants from Southern Russia. The country here is sparsely wooded, but when the road took us through some belt or clump of fir-trees, the "Yemstchik" generally took advantage of the shade to breathe his horses and adjust the "douga" (the yoke worn by the centre horse in a "troika"). He seldom lingered more than a minute, although one would, under other circumstances, willingly have wasted an hour or two in those cool, fragrant oases, listening to the drone of insects or soft, low notes of a cuckoo far away, and breathing in the fresh, pine-scented air and fragrance of violets and lilies-of-the-valley growing freely by the roadside. I say "under other circumstances," for even the beauties of nature are apt to lose much of their charm when viewed by a poor mortal tortured by hunger, and parched with thirst.

We had completed more than half the stage, and K—— was in the act of remarking that we had broken the neck of the journey to Nova-Silya, when something else of far more importance also came to pieces, namely, the hind wheel of the "Tarantass," which, after a succession of violent oscillations—for we were going at full gallop—subsided on its side, and again deposited us in the same stationary and helpless position as before. K——, who, like most Russians, was a true stoic, appeared rather amused than disconcerted by the accident.

"It is nothing," he said, taking a fowling-piece from its green baize cover, and filling his pocket with cartridges; "the 'Yemstchik' will return to Prokhori with the 'troika' for another conveyance, and we will walk on towards Spask. Who knows? We may pick up a hare for supper."

So we strolled slowly along the dusty road, through the cool evening air, but it was not till darkness had set in, and the lights of Spask were glimmering on the horizon, that the "Yemstchik," who had only succeeded in borrowing a rough country-cart, overtook us;

and eventually landed us, at 9.30 p.m., in the Post House.

Spask, once a tiny hamlet, is now a fair-sized town, having been selected as the site of important works connected with the Siberian Railway. I now found that the road from here to Boussè was an entirely new one, lately constructed for the benefit of those connected with the line, which it closely follows all the way. The Postmaster qualified this information by observing that, for all he knew, the road no longer existed, as, on the further side of Nova-Silya, it had been entirely submerged for over three weeks. Indeed, I should doubt whether, under any circumstances, it warranted the name of road, although the Oussouri end is, for about twenty miles, beautifully laid. It seemed almost as if the engineer had commenced from Boussè with the most scrupulous care and attention, and had suddenly become demoralised, taken to drink, and flinging prudence to the winds, finished it anyhow. A spirited discussion then took place between the Postmaster and K——, over a frizzling dish of fried eggs and bacon—which, I must own, interested me far more than topographical details—as to whether we could proceed to Nova-Silya that night. On this point, however, the Postmaster was adamant. The road was quite impassable on wheels, and no power on earth should induce him to let us have Government horses for saddle work. He added, however, that we could, if so disposed, hire them from a friend of his in the town. Fortified by food and several glasses of tea, I promptly fell in with K——'s proposition that we should start forthwith. A messenger was accordingly despatched, and presently returned with a scraggy, gaunt-looking bay horse, about sixteen hands high, with a hungry eye, who looked as if he had been fed on wood shavings for the last few months, and a paunchy white pony, almost lost under a huge Mexican saddle, with shoe-stirrups. K—— having appropriated the pony, I climbed, with the assistance of a grinning "Yemstchik," on to the bay, to find that my saddle had apparently been stripped for the occasion from a child's rocking-horse, and that it was utterly impossible to get my feet, or even my toes, into the tiny stirrups. Any shortcomings of this kind were, however, amply compensated for by the length of the thick, weatherbeaten reins, evidently used for driving purposes, the greater part of which I was compelled to coil up in a side-pocket. For some unknown reason, my steed was provided with a large pair of blinkers.

It was nine o'clock when we set out for Nova-Silya, ten miles distant. There was no moon, but a clear, starlit sky, which, when we emerged into the open country, rendered objects around faintly visible. A "Yemstchik" on foot accompanied us as a guide, for although K—— wished to dispense with his services, the Postmaster would not hear of it, and, as events turned out, fortunately for us. Our way for the first two miles lay through a flat, swampy plain, which the monotonous croak of myriads of frogs and the weird cry of night-birds rendered inexpressibly lonely and desolate. A few yards away, on our left, the low embankment of the railway stood darkly out against the starlit sky, while here and there the gaunt skeleton-like shape of a crane or windlass towered in the darkness. I soon noted, with some uneasiness, that the road became rougher every yard we travelled. We had scarcely covered a mile before ruts had become deep, dangerous pitfalls, and tiny puddles, miniature lakes. K——'s pony ambled along comfortably enough, but my steed was a confirmed stumbler, and had already twice blundered on to his knees, without, however, unseating me. The third time I was not so fortunate, and we both measured our length in the mud. The brute was fortunately of a mild, not to say an inert, disposition, for in falling the driving reins had bound us tightly together in indissoluble bonds that it took my two companions quite five minutes to unravel. We had barely started afresh when our guide, who was walking some distance ahead, rejoined us at a run. "We can go no further," he cried excitedly; "I can see nothing but water." The man spoke the truth, for he was wringing wet. "There is no help for it," said K——; "we must get on to the embankment;" and giving his pony a sharp cut over the quarters, he turned sharply to the left and disappeared from view, having on this occasion a considerable advantage of me, for he, at any rate, knew the road. But it was no time for hesitation, so giving my horse his head, I struck my heels into his sides and blindly followed in my friend's wake, dropping with a desperate peck into a soft, boggy piece of ground at least four feet below the roadway. Floundering through this for a few yards, the embankment shortly loomed overhead, and by dint of shouts and blows I forced my wretched animal up the steep, slippery slope, and at last gained the summit, breathless and drenched with perspiration, but (for the moment) safe.

The ground here was firmer, and although some care was necessary in avoiding the piles of rails and sleepers by the track (for none had been fixed), it was infinitely preferable to the road below, which was now no longer visible. The railway might have been laid across some large lake, for the reflection of the stars plainly showed that water now surrounded us on every side. I had more than once since starting doubted the wisdom of embarking on this wild-goose chase, but when K——, the guide, and myself were presently brought up, all standing by a yawning and impassable abyss, I felt strongly tempted to suggest a postponement of operations until the next day. Not so K——, however, who took all these incidents as a matter of course. "I know this place," he said, as though it were an object of agreeable curiosity. "They are making a bridge. We must go round, the water can't be very deep." Had it been, this narrative would probably have remained unwritten, for after several attempts to save himself my horse lit on his head (in about three feet of water) at the bottom of the embankment, and it was all I could do to coax and flog him up the opposite side.

This kind of work was becoming wearisome. K——'s watch showed (by the light of one of two remaining wax matches) that it was past midnight, and we had come (according to the "Yemstchik") exactly two and a half miles. The aquatic interlude that had just taken place, however, made me almost as unwilling to return as I had been before to proceed. It was now a case of "the devil and the deep sea." We had come to a kind of canal that runs parallel to the embankment for several miles. Across this were laid a couple of narrow planks. Somewhat to my surprise, the "Yemstchik" now suggested that we should try to regain the road. Even K——, however, showed some reluctance to riding across such a frail structure, a feat which (to do him justice) no one but a madman (or a Russian "Yemstchik") would have dreamt of attempting. So it was agreed, after some discussion, that our guide should take the horses away, while we crossed on foot. Even this was no easy operation. The thin, rickety planks bent under us until, in the centre, the water washed over our feet. But we got over safely, one by one, and seating ourselves on some iron girders, lit cigarettes with the last wax match left. Its flickering light revealed the fact that it was now, by K——'s watch, 1.30 a.m.

The sky was now overcast, and a few drops of rain pattering on my face and hands soon increased to a steady downpour, which, however, was of little consequence to one already wet to the skin with dew and perspiration. But the increasing darkness was another matter, for the very road at our feet was now invisible, much more so our guide, whom we could hear splashing helplessly about with his struggling charges in the deep mud on the opposite side of the canal. We heard him reach the fording place, where the sound of repeated blows, mingled with curses, led us to assume that the horses were highly averse to a nocturnal bath. Quite ten minutes elapsed before a loud splash announced that they had taken the water. Then there was a dead silence for a few moments, and I once thought I heard a cry for help. It was not repeated, however, and K—— and I were presently much relieved to hear the brutes splashing and snorting as they gained a foothold on the opposite bank.

"Come," said K——, "let us mount."

The feasibility of this project being only marred by a sheet of water about 100 yards across and knee-deep, we were soon in the saddle again. The poor "Yemstchik" was a sorry figure indeed, and dripping from head to foot. He had miscalculated the ford, and horses and man had been compelled to swim for it. The "Yemstchik" had received a nasty kick on the head, which accounted for the cry of distress we had heard.

The remainder of the way to Nova-Silya was now clear as far as water was concerned, though the floods had left the road in a terrible condition, and our horses floundered helplessly in thick, clinging black mud that almost reached our girths and stained like ink. Day was breaking when the little settlement came in sight, and I don't think I ever welcomed the end of a journey more, for during the last three or four miles the utter exhaustion of our horses had rendered riding impossible. Not only were the latter unable to keep their legs, but the Mexican saddle had become detached, and was now reposing in the slimy depths of the canal, while my rocking-horse appendage was little better than a mass of yellow, shapeless pulp, very much of the consistency and shape of a " Welsh rare-bit." At last, dropping with fatigue, we reached the door of K——'s comfortable cottage, and having, after some difficulty, succeeded in arousing a sleepy servant, threw ourselves at full-length on sofas in the cosy sitting-room. Several glasses of tea made their appearance as if by magic, and, too tired to change my clothes, I drew a bearskin over me and soon dropped into a delicious slumber that lasted twelve hours. And, as I fell asleep, some verses that had been running in my head all through that long, miserable ride, again occurred to me—lines by the ill-fated Australian poet, Lindsay Gordon, of whose works I have always been an ardent admirer, although I scarcely felt in the mood to-night to agree with the following sentiment:

>   No game was ever yet worth a rap
>   For a rational man to play,
>   Into which no accident, no mishap,
>   Can possibly find its way.

CHAPTER VIII.

ON THE ROAD.

I AWOKE towards evening much refreshed by the rest and resolved, if possible, to continue my journey on the morrow, although the driver of the mail for Vladivostok had passed through Nova-Silya, during my slumbers, with very discouraging news. Two-thirds of the road to Boussè were entirely submerged, and in one part between the stations of Polustiánok and Shmakovka, the water had risen to a depth of several feet. I mentally noted these euphonious names with a view of avoiding night travel in their vicinity, although the most serious obstacle seemed to lie in the fact that an edict had lately been issued by the Governor of Khabarovsk strictly prohibiting the use of post-horses for anything but the conveyance of mails. This difficulty was, however, overcome by K——, who arranged to send me on at once in a country cart, or "telega." This would, however, entail a somewhat longer delay at the post station, as I must depend on the same "troika" to take me right through to my destination.

No schoolgirl, on the eve of her first garden-party, ever turned a more anxious gaze skyward than the writer of these pages on retiring to rest that night. Everything now depended on fine, dry weather, of which the clear, starlit sky seemed to indicate a continuance. The prospect seemed even more favourable when, next morning, I was awakened by floods of dazzling sunshine streaming in through the curtainless windows. The baggage had arrived from Tchernigovka in a somewhat damaged condition, but by eleven o'clock all was ready. After partaking of the last solid meal I was likely to enjoy for many days to come, I took leave of my kind host, and starting as usual at a hand gallop, Nova-Silya had soon dwindled down to a faint, glittering speck on the dull, gray-green horizon.

I may here describe the vehicle of quaint design which was to transport my now weary

NEAR NOVA-SILYA, TRANS-SIBERIAN RAILWAY.

frame to the head of the Oussouri River. A Russian (or rather, Siberian) country cart or "telega" is best described by the well-known Siberian traveller, Dr. Henry Lansdell. He says: "A 'telega' is a roofless, seatless, springless, semi-cylindrical tumbril mounted on poles which connect two wooden axle-trees. From such a fate" (as travelling in this) "may you, gentle reader, be delivered!" and I heartily echo the Doctor's sentiments, for I could not wish my worst enemy a protracted journey in one of these torture-boxes.* There can, however, be little actual physical damage done in a "telega," for the occupant sits with his feet dangling only a few inches from the ground. An upset is therefore of little consequence, but the continual strain of clinging on, to say nothing of the violent oscillations, alternating with jolts that seem to drive the brain through your skull, exhaust the strongest man, and, long before the first stage was over, I had serious thoughts of postponing the journey and remaining at Shmakovka until a "tarantass" should be forthcoming. This, however, would have meant a delay of ten days, which I could ill afford to lose; and when I saw Shmakovka, I was not sorry that I had decided to pursue my way.

---

* "Through Siberia," by the Rev. H. Lansdell. (Sampson Low & Co., London.)

The driver of my conveyance was an ex-convict, and possessed of the most villainous countenance that it has ever been my lot to look upon, a face which the loss of one eye rendered only more diabolical. I took the precaution, towards nightfall, of ostentatiously displaying my revolver (a proceeding my companion viewed with the most supreme indifference), for he was a tall, brawny fellow, and a struggle at close quarters would have been more than awkward. "He was transported for murder," K—— said, "but he is an excellent driver;" and this, indeed, was now (from my point of view) the chief consideration.

For the first eight versts all went well, the road trending over undulating downs, well above the level of the inundated districts. The railroad was seldom out of sight, although there were few signs of activity on the line, the greater part of the work being now centred on a point further north, where the floods had washed away the embankment. As we gradually descended to the level of the plains, however, the difficulty of the journey became manifest by the appearance of the landscape, which, as far as the eye could see, presented the appearance of an archipelago of islets on a sleeping sea. One could trace a thin, snakelike line extending away to the horizon, but broken in many places by the encroaching element. This was the road, which it was absolutely impossible to travel over except at a snail's pace. It was my intention to pass the night at Polustiánok, the first stage from Nova-Silya, and eighteen versts distant. I had calculated four hours at the most for the journey, but it was not till nearly midnight that we reached the post house, after as hard and trying a journey as has ever fallen to my lot. The mud was, for the greater part of the journey, far above the horses' knees, while in many places the road had rotted into a succession of deep holes full of liquid mud, and therefore indistinguishable from sound ground. Towards sunset the "telega" had floundered bodily into one of these chasms, and it occupied more than two hours to extricate it, during which time the murderer worked waist-deep in mire with an energy for which, at starting, I should not have given him credit. I have had considerable experience of rough travel in Siberia, but I have never in my wildest moments conceived a road so bad as this. The daylight faded, and dusk was succeeded by darkness, and I would gladly have abandoned Polustiánok until the morrow and sought shelter in the hut of some friendly peasant, but not a glimmer of light was visible in any direction. This so-called road was, as I have said, newly constructed for the railway, and with the exception of the sheds doing duty for post houses, there was no human habitation this side of Boussè. K—— had fortunately provided me with tea, biscuits, and sardines, so that towards ten o'clock the murderer and I were enabled to enjoy an *al fresco* repast. The worst part of the day's work was now over, and at midnight we reached Polustiánok, which consists of a log hut eighteen feet long by twelve wide, a stable (with a roof), and a shed for the Postmaster (without one).

The interior of the guest-room was somewhat primitive, and although a pile of shavings outside the doorway (there was no door) and scent of freshly-sawn pine-wood testified to its recent erection, a glance indoors showed that the designer had not unduly embellished the interior. There was no furniture of any kind, unless a narrow plank nailed around three sides of the hut can be so described. The floor was of mud, not dry, but moist, pulpy, and suggestive of odours less fragrant than dew. Had this resting-place been unoccupied, I should have been well-satisfied, but seeing that the aforesaid plank was entirely occupied by two ladies and three infantry officers gathered around a hissing "samovar," I began to wonder how and where I was to rest my aching limbs for a few hours. I was not long in doubt, for, with true Russian hospitality, I was invited to join the group. My soddened, mud-plastered valise formed a seat, and after a few glasses of scalding tea, I felt sufficiently restored in mind and body to light a cigarette, and to forget my unpleasant experiences of the day.

My travelling acquaintances had arrived a few hours before from Boussè, and to my great relief gave encouraging accounts of the road beyond Shmakovka, the next station. Up to this point, however, a repetition of to-day's work seemed likely. It could not well be worse, and it was, at any rate, a comfort to find that the road was now open.

Further conversation elicited the fact that the younger of the ladies was a bride travelling with her husband and sister to Japan, and that the tall, distinguished-looking old gentleman with half-a-dozen orders on his breast, was General "G.," *en route* with his aide-de-camp for Vladivostok. The General had been through the Crimean campaign and Russo-Turkish war, and, under any other circumstances, would have been a delightful and entertaining companion. Russians are proverbially addicted to late hours, but the General would have sat out a regiment, man by man. When, towards three a.m., he concluded his last reminiscence concerning the late General Skobeleff and a certain white horse, the aide-de-camp and myself were, from motives of policy and politeness, the only ones awake in the place. Nor should we then have had a respite (for the scene was rapidly being shifted from the Shipka Pass to Central Asia) had not the elder lady suddenly fallen off her narrow seat from sheer exhaustion. It was then suggested (much to the General's annoyance) that a few hours of rest would revive the ladies and prepare them for their arduous journey. The light having been extinguished, I was preparing to stretch myself at full length upon the floor when a touch on the shoulder attracted my attention, and I saw the aide-de-camp, the General having disappeared. "Les dames," he whispered; "we must not sleep in here. The husband of madame is sleeping on the roof, it is cool and pleasant there — join us." As a steady drizzle had set in, however, I declined my military friend's invitation, and set out for the stables, where I could, at any rate, find shelter. But an examination of the back of the hut disclosed a tiny lean-to shed, evidently used for cooking purposes, half of which had already been appropriated by the General. Spreading out my rugs I lay down, only to find that a liquid compound (presumably slops) was slowly oozing through my furs, and that the dark, mal-odorous den was infested with vermin and clouds of mosquitoes. My companion had already lit a cigarette, philosophically remarking that sleep was out of the question. So we smoked and chatted until dawn, when slumber overtook me, speedily broken by a terrific thunderstorm accompanied by torrents of rain. This soon drove in our friends from the roof, but the "Yemstchiks" were already preparing for a start, and in another hour the party had left for Tchernigovka. I am bound to confess that I did not regret their departure, but slunk back into the now empty shed, threw myself on the floor, and slept soundly until midday, when the now familiar countenance of the assassin warned me that the "telega" was ready. Breakfast, consisting of a couple of biscuits and a cup of brackish water, did not detain me long, and by one o'clock we were well on the road to Shmakovka.

Anticipation is, in this world, usually better or worse than realisation. In this instance it proved the former, for the day's drive presented but few of the difficulties, and none of the dangers, of the previous day. Yesterday we had passed through miles upon miles of flooded country, and floundered helplessly in an almost impassable morass; to-day the road was for the most part hard and dry, and but little water was to be seen around. Yesterday we had not seen a single human being, to-day scarcely an hour passed that we did not meet parties of soldiers and others repairing the railway embankment. Logs, branches, and large stones, were being hurled into the road pell-mell to preserve it from utter annihilation, while in some parts the embankment had fallen away altogether, apparently beyond the reach of repair. I could not help reflecting (and experienced engineers afterwards told me) that this part of the line must ever remain a thorn in the side of the constructors. Do what they will, Lake Khanka must ever seriously menace the welfare of the Siberian Railway, for it is practically impossible to drain the enormous territory it so frequently and fatally overflows.

The post house of Shmakovka, which we reached soon after five, was more habitable than my last resting-place. It was of substantial appearance, the wooden walls being thickly plastered with mud to keep out the cold (and, as the murderer facetiously remarked, keep in the fleas). The tiny guest-room, a stuffy little apartment, was blocked up by the mail: twenty to thirty heavily-padlocked, travel-worn leather bags, over which a dirty, forbidding-looking ruffian in dingy uniform was keeping guard, revolver in hand. In strange contrast to these grim surroundings was a young woman, reclining at full length on a long wicker chair, evidently her own property; a delicate-looking, well-dressed little person, who looked as if she had suddenly dropped from the clouds, or been transported by her evil genius from some scene of luxury and refinement to this filthy Siberian post house. I subsequently discovered that Madame D—— was, like my friend of the previous night, a bride who had only left European Russia a short time previously to share the home of her husband, a Government official at Khabarovsk. A delay of three days had, she told me, exhausted her patience, and Siberia was a name she would remember to the end of her days. I could well believe it. Her husband, a mild-eyed, heavy-looking youth, woke up at this juncture and opined that it was time to be starting, and as Madame's reply was by no means of a polite or conciliatory nature, I took my leave.

Strolling out to witness the departure of the mail, I came upon the murderer, moodily watching the proceedings from a distant corner of the yard. " Will the ' Barin ' go on to-day ? " he asked as I approached. My doubts concerning the wisdom of such a proposal were met by a smile which, though meant to be engaging, would have terrified any child of average intelligence into a fit. "Leave it to me, I will get you there," said my friend, lurching off to the stables, and emerging in less than ten minutes with the "troika" ready for the road. If my taciturn friend was guilty in the past of many misdeeds, he possessed at any rate one redeeming virtue, that, especially in Siberia, covers a multitude of sins. He knew the value of time.

The road improved every hour after leaving Shmakovka, for here the floods had entirely receded. Four days of cloudless weather had dried up the track, leaving, however, huge cracks and fissures that more than once brought us to grief. The jolting now became so violent and incessant that I found it impossible to keep a cigarette between my teeth, and my hands were soon sore and blistered from holding on to the rough sides of the "telega." But the worst was now over, and nearing Rijova, the next station, we passed through some really beautiful scenery. The northern sky-line was now broken by a range of wooded hills, beyond which lay the head waters of the Oussouri River and my destination, Boussè. Far behind us the treacherous marshes were lost in gray mist, and the sight of green, undulating pastures with cattle browsing knee-deep, in rippling, fern-fringed brooks sparkling in the sunshine, and the sweet scent of thousands of wild flowers, inspired a sense of rest and comfort that I had not experienced since leaving the sea. Nearing the end of the stage, we passed a large caravan of horses from Tomsk, on their way to Vladivostok. They are bigger than the cattle in these parts, and are prized accordingly for town purposes, although for rough country work they are not to be compared to the small, wiry animals that had brought me along. Some of these must have stood quite sixteen hands, and were well-shaped and good looking. They left us a *souvenir* in the shape of some huge horse-flies that nearly maddened our team and inflicted a nasty, poisonous bite on hands and face. This was merely a foretaste of what was to follow, for we passed through clouds of them for the remainder of the journey; and suffered accordingly.

A quiet night's rest in the clean, roomy post house at Rijova, following a substantial and welcome meal of eggs and black bread, reconciled me to all the dirt and discomfort of the past four days; and although here, as elsewhere, the mosquitoes* were troublesome, and the horse-flies had left some painful, irritating wounds, I slept as soundly as though my aching bones were reposing, not on bare boards, but clean sheets and a soft, yielding mattress.

A drive of about ten miles in brilliant sunshine and glorious scenery brought us to the banks of the Oussouri River, when our "telega" was placed on the ferry and conveyed across, not without some difficulty, for

---

* I may here remark, for the benefit of sufferers, that "essential oil of cloves," with a due proportion of water, is an excellent preventive against these pests.

the stream, about a quarter of a mile in breadth, is both rapid and dangerous. A large stone bridge (about half finished) was here in course of construction, though work had been abandoned for some time, probably on account of the floods. At Kazarm, a few miles further on, quite 1,000 soldiers were employed on an embankment, cheery, ruddy-looking fellows clad in linen, and huge, white flat caps, with which Vereschagin's war pictures have made us familiar. A party of officers, distinguishable by their gold shoulder-straps, were superintending the work, and evidently did not relish the occupation. There was a tiny post house here, pleasantly situated in a shady grove of pines, and having now only seven miles to accomplish, I gave the horses a rest and a much-needed feed of corn, and secured some milk and black bread for my own consumption. The murderer, having found an old acquaintance among the "Yemstchiks," disappeared, and did not return for a considerable time. When he at length put in an appearance, a marked change in his demeanour, and the powerful odour of alcohol emanating from his person, soon convinced me (and correctly) that there was a brandy shop not far distant. The rouble that I had advanced my friend that morning for the purchase of food, had evidently been laid out in a very different manner.

A kind Providence usually watches over the doings of drunken men, or I might never have reached Boussè. For the first two or three miles our course was so erratic that I thought more than once of completing the journey on foot, for my Jehu showed an utter disregard to the direction taken by his team. Interference might, by suddenly attracting his attention, have meant an upset, so I resignedly and silently watched his antics, which, for the first part of the stage, were confined to a long conversation with his horses, alternating with wild bursts of song: "Oh, my darlings! My little brothers! My white pigeons! How cruel to bring you through such an awful country! But never mind, the Barin is good—he will give us drink — plenty of drink at Boussè. Ah! you would, you son of a pig's father!" And a stinging blow from the heavy whip was heard as one of the "troika" stumbled from sheer leg-weariness on to his head. "I will teach you—and you—and you" (accompanying each word with a resounding cut), "how to keep on your rickety legs." This performance usually ended in a furious gallop, which, though like the donkey's, was generally short and sweet, once so nearly culminated in an upset that I was forced to remonstrate. This evidently wounded my companion's feelings, for he relapsed into a sulky silence, and our mad career suddenly dropped from an honest fifteen miles an hour to an uncertain crawl, gradually dwindling down to a standstill, which was scarcely surprising seeing that this strange weird being had dropped into a peaceful slumber.

So we travel on until dusk, when our "troika" crawls more dead than alive into the little village of Boussè, where I am met by the cheerful intelligence that the weekly steamer had left for Khabarovsk on the previous day. Bidding farewell to my still inebriated friend I enter the little post house and spread out my rugs for a lengthened stay, after as disagreeable, difficult, and exhausting a journey as it has ever fallen to my lot (even in Siberia) to accomplish.

CHAPTER IX.

THE OUSSOURI AND AMOUR RIVERS. BOUSSÈ— KHABAROVSK.

BOUSSÈ, which contains about 500 inhabitants, is picturesquely situated on the banks of the Oussouri River, and is the terminus of the river steamers that, in summer, ply between the head waters of the Amour River* and Vladivostok. It is a pretty, homely-looking village, and its neatly built log-huts and well-kept gardens are a pleasing contrast to the usual Siberian *coup d'œil* of neglect and squalor. The post house was outwardly clean and commodious, but the guest-room in which

---

* Derived from the Manchu word "Yamour," "Great River." The total length of the Amour River is 3,066 miles, with a fall of 6,000 feet.

I was fated to reside: for at least a week was a fusty, unclean apartment, swarming with rats and "tarakans" (a species of small cockroach), which towards evening swarmed in thousands from crevices in the walls and flooring. The furniture consisted of a small table, a hard wooden chair, and a still harder bench which formed a resting-place during the night. One must not be particular in Siberia, and I should not have complained had my privacy not been rudely disturbed (within a few hours) by the married couple from Shmakovka. These were closely followed by a succession of belated wayfarers, until there was scarcely breathing room in the tiny, mal-odorous den. Eating became an impossibility, while sleep would have meant asphyxiation.

Beyond Boussè, the right bank of the Oussouri and Amour Rivers, as far as the confluent of the Shilka, is inhabited by so-called "Cossacks." I say "so-called," because there is little in the origin, mode of life, or even organisation of these people to justify even their comparison with the hardy, warlike tribes of the Don and Oural. When Russia took possession of the Amour provinces it became necessary to take defensive precautions and, if possible, to colonise the newly acquired districts. General Mouravieff (then Governor-General of Khabarovsk) decided (probably on economical grounds) to select a number of convicts from Eastern Siberia, station them twenty to thirty versts along the Amour and Oussouri Rivers, and form them into "Sótnias" or hundreds in the Cossack style. A small remuneration and so much flour and other provisions per month is now allowed them on their undertaking to serve as soldiers (should their services be needed) from twenty-five to forty-five years of age. The number of these men has been greatly increased of late years by emigrants from European Russia and Western Siberia, but it is scarcely probable that they would prove of much service against a civilised force. The Cossack of the Oussouri is simply a ploughboy in uniform, and derives his name of "Cossack" chiefly from the yellow-striped breeches, rifle and "Nagaika"* he receives from the Government. As settlers the inhabitants of the Oussouri Valley are a lamentable failure. Although supplied by the Government with agricultural implements, cattle and horses, while the splendid crops of hay and cereals grown by the "Mandzas" or Chinese emigrants, testify to the excellence of the soil, the lazy Russian colonists utterly decline to work, and so long as they can grow a sufficient quantity of potatoes for home consumption, are quite content to idle their lives away.

It is weary work at any time waiting for a train or steamer, but I fancy my enforced sojourn at Boussè would have tried the patience of Job himself. My library consisted (as usual on these lengthened journeys, where weight is a consideration) of a "Whitaker's Almanack" for the current year, and a tattered Shakespeare. But the glory of the latter was somewhat

---

* Cossack whip.

dimmed by Siberian surroundings and (I am ashamed to add) an empty stomach, and, long before the welcome whistle was heard, I had, by the aid of the Almanack, mastered the dates of every important event from the Flood downwards, to say nothing of the statistics of the most obscure Republic in Central America. On the second day some excitement was caused by the arrival of the newly married couple from Shmakovka, but the joy attendant on the sight of a new face was speedily qualified by the reflection that here, as at Polustiánok, I might be requested to pass the night outside, upon the roof. Madame, however, was on this occasion more considerate, and, although she and her spouse appropriated my sleeping place (the bench) of the previous night, I was permitted to retire to rest with the rats and "tarakans" on the filthy floor. I should perhaps have fared better outside, for sleep was rendered impossible by the repeated attacks of these latter pests, who inflict a nasty poisonous bite. Miniature embankments of Keating's powder around the legs of the bench had repulsed them on the previous evening, but they now attacked me in myriads, and I arose next day with face and hands raw with bites. I have since invariably slept in gloves, a habit I would recommend to all travellers in these regions.

The new arrivals were pleasant people enough. Madame spoke French and sang sweetly, and her husband was a sociable, intelligent fellow, but I should have appreciated their society far more had the contents of the post larder been less restricted. When, on the fourth day, three more travellers put in an appearance, eggs and bread were at a premium. On the sixth day, it was scarcely possible to procure food at all. My only meal on the seventh, or last day, consisted of a small piece of black bread, two venerable-looking eggs of dubious flavour (purchased in the village), and an onion, furtively abstracted from the post house garden, and eaten raw.

So the long sunny days crawled slowly by in dreary monotony. There was literally nothing to do but to stroll aimlessly down to the riverside a few yards distant, and back again, while, towards evening, the operation of watering the little garden outside the guest-room was watched with positive interest by the disgusted inmates, glad of any pretext to divert the mind. But at last, one propitious morning just before sunrise, when, owing to the unusual activity of "tarakans," I had lain awake all night, the welcome sound of a distant whistle broke the stillness. Dreading disappointment, I lay for some moments in eager expectancy, till the rhythmical beat of paddles banished all doubt, and I rushed to the window to see the familiar red and green lights moving slowly up the river in the gray dawn. An hour later I was comfortably installed alone in a little white cabin glistening with paint and varnish, and at midday sat down to an excellent *déjeuner* that quite equalled, if it did not excel, the fare on board a Rhine or Danube steamboat. The enjoyment of coffee and cigarettes under the deck awning was only enhanced by a distant view of the dirty post house, for the pleasures of this life are as comparative as they are, unfortunately, brief.* By the time we were under way, our new and luxurious surroundings had grown familiar, and the unsavoury reminiscences of the past few days had almost entirely faded from memory.

The *Graf Putiyatin* was one of a fleet of twenty-five vessels known as the "Amour Steam Navigation Company." The latter is of recent origin, its promoters having bought up the dirty, slow-going wooden tubs that formerly carried the mails and replaced them by fine, speedy iron boats built by Messrs. Cockerill & Co., of Belgium. Although the *Graf Putiyatin* was replete with every comfort, she was one of the smallest boats on the line, the larger ones being kept solely for the services between Blagovieshtchensk and Nikolaefsk, for the Amour, north of Khabarovsk, sometimes gets up a very nasty sea, in which a small river boat would stand a poor chance.

We had for a time escaped from the torments of "tarakans," but mosquitoes soon became very troublesome both by day and by night. A species of small sandfly also attacked us in the marshy regions and inflicted a poisonous bite. But these are minor annoyances after real hardships, and glorious weather and pleasant fellow-travellers amply atoned for them. Just before leaving Boussè, we were joined by General Grodékoff (of Herat fame), who was returning to Khabarovsk after a tour of inspection on his appointment as Deputy-Governor of the Amour Provinces. The General, his aide-de-camp, and M. and Mdme. B—— (the newly-married pair) constituted our party, which was just large enough to make things sociable. This part of my journey was perhaps, from beginning to end, the most enjoyable. But, like most enjoyable things, it did not last long.

A lengthened stay at most of the stations afforded plenty of opportunity of studying the natives and their surroundings, and of replenishing our larder with fresh fish (for the river teems with carp, starlet, and salmon), game, and ice. The villages on the banks of the

Oussouri River are chiefly peopled by the Cossacks of whom I have spoken, but the indigenous race of these regions is known as the Goldi. The latter number about 5,000 in all, and inhabit the Amour as far as the Gilyak country on the north, extending on the south as far as the Upper Oussouri. The Goldi are of Mongolian descent, and, like the Gilyaks, shave their heads with the exception of a small pig-tail. Unlike the latter, however, they are rapidly becoming Russianised and increase, if anything, in numbers. The Goldi do not cultivate as a rule, but subsist on millet and rice, which they procure in exchange for furs. Perhaps the most interesting feature of the Oussouri River is the queer mixture of races on either side: the stolid, sunburnt Russian and his rosy-cheeked *frau*, and uncanny-looking, ragged Goldi on the one bank, and on the other, the blue-clad, yellow-faced Manchu, with his pig-tail, fan, painted, doll-faced women, and generally celestial surroundings. The dwellings contrasted as strangely as their inhabitants:

the Russian *Izbas* on the right bank, and Chinese-looking habitations opposite, clearly marking the frontier-line of the two greatest empires in the world.

On the third day, at Koslovski, one of the largest stations, preparations had been made for General Grodékoff's reception by the *ataman*, or, in Cossack parlance, headman of the village, and, being a *prasnik* or public holiday, the population had turned out *en masse* to witness the ceremony. Koslovski is a picturesque village of seventy to eighty houses, and the bright red "kaftans" of the men and gaily-dressed women formed a pleasing sight in the brilliant sunshine. The *ataman*, who was attired in full uniform, was followed by an attendant bearing a huge loaf of black bread and a saucer of salt on a tray covered by a snowy napkin. Having partaken of this, the General led the way, followed at a respectful distance by the *ataman*, and we walked slowly through the village, a crowd of young men and girls bringing up the rear. The church, the *ataman's* house, and the school were visited in turn. I was surprised, in the latter, at the intelligence shown by some of the younger boys. This was the more remarkable in that it is only within the past two or three years that education in these districts has been made compulsory. The school children looked healthy, happy, and contented, like every one else in the place, for these people pay no taxes, have no care for the morrow, and are well cared for by the Government. Here, as in every other *stanitza** we passed, I noticed a large black board erected in a prominent position near the landing-place. On it appeared, in white letters, the following record:

KOSLOVSKI STANITZA.

Houses	73
Men	145
Women	143
Non-commissioned officers	4
Horses	340
Cattle	272
Land under cultivation	202 acres.

---

* The Cossack term for "village."

Although General Grodékoff was enthusiastic in his praises of Khabarovsk, his aide-de-camp, Lieutenant V——, a cavalry officer, who had been quartered there for over two years, did not share his chief's favourable opinions. The life, according to the Lieutenant, was terribly monotonous in summer, while in winter it became absolutely unbearable to those lucky beings who could afford to move to more congenial climes. The common necessaries of life were outrageously dear, and, as Russian officers are notoriously underpaid, it became at times extremely difficult to make both ends meet, especially to those warriors not blessed with private means. My informant was in receipt of only £120 a year all told. On this he was expected to keep a horse and to live and look like a gentleman. His Colonel was little better off, being a married man with an establishment to keep up on £300 per annum. A Lieutenant of the line is even worse off, drawing £84, with no extras or allowances whatever.

Nearing Khabarovsk, the Oussouri widens considerably, and, at its junction with the large river, presents the appearance of a huge lake dotted with numerous islands. The scenery around Kaza-Kévitch, the last station, somewhat resembled an English landscape, with its long stretches of down-land, thickly wooded valleys, and silvery streams, alternating with dark patches of ploughed land. Towards midday, on the 9th of June, we entered the broad, swiftly-flowing Amour, and an hour later Khabarovsk, still miles away, a dab of gray on a green hillside, came in sight. "Khabarovsk," "Oussouri," "l'Amour,"* said the General, genially quoting the *bon mot* of a French traveller, and surveying the distant city through a field-glass. "Does it?" growled the aide-de-camp in an undertone, and turning on his heel with a look of disgust.

---

* "Khabarovsk où sourit l'amour."

CHAPTER X.

THE UPPER AMOUR AND SHILKA RIVERS.
KHABAROVSK—STRETYNSK.

WERE I condemned to pass the rest of my days in Siberia (which Heaven forbid!), I should certainly select Khabarovsk as a residence. My friend Lieut. V—— was evidently a pessimist, for my first impressions of the place were decidedly favourable, the more so that Khabarovsk has not the depressing influence of most Siberian towns. There are several fine brick buildings, and most of the wooden houses are whitewashed, while the principal street, a broad, well-kept thoroughfare, is laid out like a *boulevard*, the dwellings on either side being fronted by flower gardens. There are good shops, a club, street conveyances, a weekly newspaper, and even a theatre, but, as usual, no hotel; and this is the capital of a province more than three times the size of France! This difficulty, however, was overcome by an invitation to remain on board the *Graf Putiyatin* until the arrival of the steamer from Nikolaefsk, so caused me little inconvenience.

The city of Khabarovsk was founded by General Mouravieff in the year 1858. The original name of Khabarovka* was derived from that of a Cossack chief, Khabarof, who towards the middle of the seventeenth century descended the Amour River at the head of an expedition. The town, which contains about 14,000 inhabitants, stands on a promontory overlooking an immense sheet of water formed by the confluence of the two rivers, and is one day destined to become, both commercially and strategically, a most important place, being equidistant from Vladivostok, Blagovieshtchensk and Nikolaefsk. Khabarovsk is not only the seat of the Government of the vast Amour and Primorski

---

* Now changed to Khabarovsk.

districts, which include Kamchatka and the Trans-Baikal regions, but it is also strongly garrisoned. It contained, at the time of my visit, a military force of over 2,000 men, comprising a battalion of infantry, a battalion of Siberian riflemen, and a brigade of artillery, but the strength has since been largely increased. There are no fortifications as yet, but the position could easily be made a very strong one. During the summer trade is brisk. At least ten steamers ply on the Amour, where twenty years ago one sufficed. The same may be said of the rivers of Western Siberia, where the traffic has increased from 40,000 tons in 1886 to 320,000 tons in 1892. Navigation on the Amour is closed from October until May, during which time sleighs are employed for transport of passengers and merchandise along the frozen river. The winter journey to St. Petersburg can be made in about six weeks, travelling night and day. It is difficult to realise that the thermometer here sometimes falls to 20 degrees below zero, for the heat was tropical and sun so powerful

PANORAMA OF KHABAROVSK.

that it was dangerous to venture out at midday without head protection.

An invitation on the second day of my stay to dine with the Governor-General was somewhat embarrassing, for the graceful appearance of a dress suit is not enhanced by contrast with a gray flannel shirt. Starch had long ceased to interest me, and white collars were a thing of the past. So I was compelled to ransack the shops in search of a ready-made article, but with the exception of some gaily-striped "dickies," could find nothing to meet my requirements. I had, therefore, no alternative but to present myself in travelling costume, but was soon reassured by my hosts, who declared that they had never expected me to appear in any other garb. And although, at first, the brilliant uniforms and smart dinner gowns gave one somewhat the feeling that a painted rat must experience, who has been turned loose to scare his fellows, the kindly welcome extended me by the Governor-General and his charming wife, would under any circumstances have made one feel at home.

We adjournéd to the garden after dinner, for the evenings at this time of the year are cool and pleasant and the twilight long. Among the guests was Lieutenant Philimónoff of the Engineers, an agreeable, amusing fellow, who spoke French fluently. He was returning immediately to Europe, overland, and I was glad to find that we were to travel together by the same steamer as far as Stretynsk. Music and dancing wound up a very enjoyable evening, and, at parting, the Governor-General handed me the credentials authorising me to visit the penal establishments under his jurisdiction. The following is an English translation of this document, which ran as follows:

"By Order.

"The bearer, Mr. Harry de Windt, an English subject, has arrived in the Amour Provinces with the intention of studying our penal establishments and exile system.

"This is to command all Governors of prisons and jails throughout the Amour District to afford Mr. de Windt every facility in examining the establishments under their care, and to provide him with all the details that he may require.

"I hereby also command the officers of all grades of the Police to afford Mr. de Windt every assistance of which he may stand in need.

"(Signed)   DOUKHOVSKOY,
"General Governor of the Amour Provinces,
"Eastern Siberia.

"Khabarovsk, June 9th, 1894."

That the instructions contained in the above were afterwards carried out to the letter the reader will presently see for himself.

The *Baron Korff* was advertised to leave at noon, but it was nearly sunset before the big white steamer cast off from the landing-stage. I embarked, on her arrival, at eight a.m., and was somewhat surprised to find that the captain was entertaining a large luncheon party

P

at midday. The ladies at this entertainment belonged chiefly to the middle class, although I noticed many of my male acquaintances of the previous evening. Among the latter was Philimónoff, whose brother officers had come to bid him adieu. Champagne flowed like water, and vodka like wine, for at least an hour before the banquet, which circumstance, aided by a blazing sun and overpowering heat, would probably have had a disastrous effect on ordinary mortals. But Russian soldiers can scarcely be counted as such (especially as regards alcoholic consumption), and, although I felt anything but comfortable, my military friends sat down to lunch as coolly and serenely as if they had subsisted for the past month or so on a diet of toast and water. The feminine element was represented by the wives and daughters of the under officials and tradesmen, and were, to say the least of it, not prepossessing. Most of them looked as if they had walked out of a fashion plate of the year 1860, while others younger and more up to date reminded one painfully of Albert Chevalier's heroines of Hampstead and the Old Kent Road, with their gaudy, ill-fitting dresses and huge feathered hats. But habit is everything, and these plain, frowzy-looking damsels received almost as much attention from the Governor-General's staff as any Court beauty at Gatchina or the Winter Palace.

The *Baron Korff* was a fine, roomy paddle-wheel steamer, built of iron and decked over with the same material, the passenger accommodation consisting of a wooden deck-house forward of the engines. She was 250 feet long, capable of steaming a good ten knots against a strong current, and drew, when fully loaded, only four feet, as the Amour is in places extremely shallow, and for the greater part of the journey a man was stationed in the bows sounding with a long pole. The distance from Khabarovsk to Blagovieshtchensk is 845 versts, and there are thirty-one stations, of which the pretty town of Michaelo-Semonovsk (named after a former Governor of

Eastern Siberia) is the largest. The Amour, for a considerable distance above Khabarovsk, presents the appearance of a series of huge lakes through which, in thick weather, it is sometimes very puzzling to find a way. Even on a bright clear day an outlet is often invisible, to the inexperienced eye, for hours together. When the river narrowed we travelled night and day, and the navigation after dark was sometimes anything but reassuring. There is no rule of the road, but when two vessels meet, a red or green light is waved from the bridge to indicate the course they intend steering, a vague signal that sometimes leads (as in our case) to fatal results.

I was glad to find, when we had at length fairly started, that although the second class was crowded to suffocation, and the decks thronged with peasantry, there were still some first-class cabins vacant. We sat down five to supper, including Colonel Pakatilo, a bearded giant quartered at Khabarovsk, and his young wife, Monsieur Yordansky, the proprietor of a gold mine on the Zeya River, a tributary of the Amour, Philimónoff, and myself. Conversation was chiefly carried on in French, and these pleasant companions lightened, to a great extent, the monotony of the journey, especially Madame Pakatilo, who was the life and soul of the party. But even this bright little lady succumbed at last to the universal boredom, for, when the novelty has worn off, there are few things so dreary and depressing as river travel in Siberia. So the hours crowded by with exasperating slowness for every one but Yordansky and Philimónoff, who were passionately addicted to "Vint."* The *Baron Korff* stopped at nearly every station for the purpose of taking or discharging passengers and cargo, and loading fuel. The latter consists of pine-logs, and emitted a shower of sparks and flowing cinders from our funnels which often made me tremble for the safety of the ship, to say nothing of the fact that my clothes

---

* Russian whist.

were honeycombed with holes when we arrived at Stretynsk. Landing at the stations was not always easy, being generally effected across a narrow plank laid from the deck, and ending, as a rule, on a steep, slippery mud-bank. But a stroll ashore was always worth the risk of a wetting, and we usually returned from these expeditions laden with wild flowers, with which Madame Pakatilo embellished the saloon table, or a welcome addition to our menu in the shape of wild strawberries and clotted cream. Game is generally plentiful on Siberian rivers, and I was surprised at its scarcity on the Amour. On the other hand, fish of all kinds was both cheap and easily obtainable. Ice, too, was procurable at most of the villages, which, the weather being tropical, was indeed a blessing. I have seldom experienced such heat, even in India, but although the days were stifling, the evenings were cool and delicious, and a cigar on the still, starlit deck in a night air laden with the scent of pines, dewy grass, and flowers compensated for many evils. The mosquitoes, too, which were troublesome enough at midday, disappeared at sundown, and permitted one to sleep in peace, so, as regards personal comfort, there was really little to complain of.

We passed, shortly after leaving Khabarovsk, the mouth of the Soungari River, which, with its affluents, drains a large portion of Manchuria. It is navigable as far as Girin, a large city where we heard that an insurrection had just broken out which might lead to serious complications. The valley of the Soungari is fertile and well populated, but seldom visited by Russians, although a large trade in cereals is done by the Chinese. The grain is brought in junks from the Tsi-Cheng district, and during the summer season over 150,000 pouds* finds its way to Khabarovsk and Blagovieshtchensk, the wheat fetching forty kopeks and the rice one rouble and twenty kopeks per poud. To facilitate the transport the Chinese

---

* A poud is thirty-six English pounds.

traders offered to buy a couple of steamers from a Khabarovsk merchant, but although the latter was willing to sell, the Russian Government would not sanction the scheme, fearing that this might form the nucleus of a Celestial fleet that might some day, for obvious reasons, prove troublesome.

The scenery above this was of the most dreary description, consisting chiefly of low mudbanks, thickly covered with dense forest, while inland, impenetrable swamps stretched away for miles on every side. Towards Skobeltzina, however, the outlook improved, and mountains once more gladdened the eye and relieved the monotonous landscape of the past few days. At this station (about 230 versts from Blagovieshtchensk) the Bureya River flows in from the north, a distance of over 700 miles, and we passed through some glorious scenery at a point where the mountains of the same name cross the Amour Valley. Coal seams of considerable thickness have been discovered near here, and a spot just below the station has been rendered historical by the fact that a bear, while attempting to swim across the river, was shot there by the Tsarevitch in 1891.

Nearing Blagovieshtchensk, the weather broke up, and cloudless skies were replaced by dense mists and drizzling rain. On the third day we reached, towards evening, the small station of Konstantinovsk, and having loaded fuel, resumed our journey in the twilight. The rain, which had fallen steadily all day, had ceased for a time, and thin rifts of blue appeared in the western sky, where the sun was sinking below the horizon like a ball of fire, and casting lurid rays over the placid, silvery river. Supper was just over, Madame Pakatilo was engrossed in the pages of a yellow-backed French novel, and Yordansky and Philimónoff deep, as usual, in the intricacies of "Vint," so I retired to my cabin to jot down the events of the day. Scarcely, however, had I put pen to paper than a terrible, grinding crash shook the vessel from stem to stern, overturned the candle, and threw me to the ground in the darkness. At the same moment the whistle sounded, rising shrilly above the screams of women and children and the hurried tramp of men. Groping my way, with some difficulty, to the door, I threw it open on a scene of the wildest confusion, which the roar of escaping steam did not tend to diminish. The panic-stricken deck passengers had gathered together forward, and were rushing madly from side to side in such numbers, that I fully expected an upset. Colonel Pakatilo was standing at the saloon entrance, brandishing his sword, and alternately threatening and imploring the unruly crowd to keep calm in a voice that might have been heard at Konstantinovsk—ten versts away. It was now pouring in torrents, and seeing Madame Pakatilo cowering alone against the deck-house and sobbing bitterly, I ran back to my cabin for a fur cloak and enveloped the poor little shivering figure in its warm folds. I then fought my way through the throng of terrified moujiks to the bridge, where Yordansky and Philimonoff were calmly surveying the scene.

We had, they informed me, collided with a steamer, the *Shilka*, cutting her down to the water's edge. She was rapidly sinking, but the damage sustained by the *Baron Korff* had not yet been ascertained. "The captain says we are safe for at least ten minutes," said Philimónoff, coolly lighting a cigarette, "and that if the worst is realised, he will beach the steamer." As the latter was now in mid-stream of a terrific current, quite half a mile from either bank, without even a life-belt, to say nothing of a boat, on board, this information was more or less reassuring. The captain himself then appeared, with the welcome news that our injury was slight, but that the *Shilka* was slowly settling down. Confidence having been restored by this announcement from the bridge, I descended and made my way to the bows, which were still firmly embedded in the side of the sinking steamer. The dim light of a flickering lantern showed that a plank had been thrown between the two boats, which enabled the passengers and crew to escape, but the *Shilka* also carried a number of horses, whose neighs of terror were pitiful to hear. Although the collision had only slightly twisted our bows, the water was rushing like a mill-sluice into the rent cut by the *Baron Korff*. By dint, however, of forging slowly ahead, our captain managed to ground both vessels gently on an adjacent sandbank, and when the *Shilka* finally sank it was only in six feet of water, which left her decks dry. The horses were swum ashore next morning without much difficulty, and the steamer herself eventually raised and repaired. Such incidents are of common occurrence on the Amour, but the accident was undoubtedly due to the erratic system of night-signalling on that river that I have already described.

Shortly after we had grounded in safety it was discovered that a terrible catastrophe had happened. One of the firemen was suddenly missed, and, a search being made, was found crushed to death in his bunk, which was situated exactly at the spot where our bows had entered the iron plates of the *Shilka*, forcing them inwards upon the occupant, and mutilating him in a shocking manner. The poor fellow had been jammed in so tightly that it was almost impossible to extricate him from the *débris* of twisted metal and splintered wood. Death must happily have been instantaneous, for although nearly every bone was crushed into fragments, and the body terribly distorted, the features were as calm and composed as those of a sleeping child. It is more than fortunate that the collision took place at dusk. Had it occurred at midnight, I doubt whether even Pakatilo's stern demeanour and stentorian voice would have averted a fatal panic, with serious loss of life.

Starting at dawn the next day, we passed Aigun, on the Manchurian bank, about four o'clock the same afternoon. This city was formerly the capital of the Chinese province of the Amour, and contains over 20,000 inhabitants. It consists of a large mud fort, a perfect warren of houses of the same material, and many gaily-painted temples and bell-encircled pagodas. The town is surrounded by emerald green plains of wheat and barley, interspersed with dark belts of pine forest, while a serrated chain of mountains breaks the sky-line to the south. The river banks were lined with junks, and the dark narrow streets swarming with people in strange barbaric costumes, gaudy banners, and shop signs glistening with vermilion and gold, presenting a striking contrast to a quiet, peaceful-looking Russian village just over the river. It was like a bit of China let into Switzerland. The trade of Aigun is considerable, and there is a caravan road leading direct from here to Pekin, viâ Tsitsihar.

Aigun is about twenty miles from Blagovieshtchensk, and by seven o'clock we had reached our destination and were safely moored at the *Pristain*, or principal landing-place. Philimónoff and I here bade adieu to our fellow-passengers, Colonel Pakatilo insisting on the consumption of a *punch d'honneur* as a stirrup-cup, which Yordansky, who was leaving immediately for his mine on the Zeya River, unfortunately could not join in. The Zeya flows into the Amour a short distance below Blagovieshtchensk, and although its course is over 700 miles, is nearly a mile wide at its affluence with the larger river. The enormous volume of water discharged by the Zeya sometimes floods the town of Blagovieshtchensk to a depth of several feet. The banks are populated by about 5,000 peasants, some of whom are employed in gold mining, although the soil is extremely fertile. Yordansky's mines are situated about 400 versts from the mouth, and my friend informed me that he had, in one year, realised 40 pouds* of gold with 212 workmen. Small nuggets have also been found. All gold obtained by private individuals in Siberia has to be sent to the Government smelting houses, of which there are two, one for Western Siberia at Tomsk, and one for

---

* A poud is thirty-six English pounds.

Eastern Siberia at Irkoutsk. The gold is smelted, and its degree of purity determined by assay. It is then forwarded to the mint at St. Petersburg, and the finders are given bills by which they obtain gold or silver coin in proportion to the value received.

Foreigners of any nationality are scarce in Siberia, and I was surprised to find a Frenchman among the holiday-makers (for it was a Sunday) assembled to witness the arrival of the *Baron Korff*. Monsieur du Roché was a Parisian, a native of Montmartre, and his clear, crisp accent seemed to land one at a jump in the fair French city so far away. I was only too glad to accept my new acquaintance's invitation to partake of a *Bock* at a building, dignified by the name of hotel, which adjoined the landing-place. A cool, shady garden surrounded the inn, and here supper was served *al fresco* while my host discoursed upon Blagovieshtchensk, its inhabitants and customs. Monsieur du Roché was a photographer, and had lived here for seven years. He was now returning to France, having amassed a considerable sum of money, for his art is popular in the smallest Siberian towns. So we sat on chatting, and smoking, and discussing our *Bock* (which, by the way, was a local product and delicious) till the stars were twinkling overhead, and it was time to return to the steamer to make preparations for an early start next morning.

Blagovieshtchensk, a name signifying in the Russian language "Annunciation," was founded in the year 1858, and is a picturesque town of about 20,000 inhabitants. The population has greatly increased of late years, for when Dr. Lansdell visited the place in 1878, it did not contain a quarter of this number. Many of the buildings are of whitewashed brick, and while the principal streets are lined with trees, the houses of the wealthier classes are embowered in shrubs and flowers. The greenery and gardens convey to the stranger the impression of an untidy, unpaved German watering-place, say Homburg or Wiesbaden, without the "Kursaals," comforts, or—hotels. Here, as at Khabarovsk, the light colour of the soil conduces greatly to the cheerful appearance of the broad, straggling streets, in which there are good shops, a theatre, and a circus. I was told that the latter, although ten years old, had only once served as a place of entertainment, but the former is frequently engaged by strolling players. Blagovieshtchensk is the seat of a Vice-Governor, a subordinate of the Governor-General at Khabarovsk, and was garrisoned, at the time of my visit, by a regiment of Siberian Cossacks, an infantry regiment, and a battery of artillery. There is a considerable amount of trade here during the summer months. Goods from Europe are invariably brought to Blagovieshtchensk by land, across Siberia, while supplies for Khabarovsk are imported, viâ Vladivostok, by sea.

Blagovieshtchensk is the terminus for the larger steamers of the Amour Company. Owing to the shallowness of the Upper Amour and Shilka Rivers, only steamers of very light draught can ascend the stream higher than Blagovieshtchensk on even ordinary occasions. An unusually dry season had now rendered it impossible to proceed to Stretynsk by the regular boat, and we were, therefore, compelled to embark on a flat-bottomed barge towed by a small tug drawing only a couple of feet. The change was not for the better, the *Psyche*, our new home, being only eighty feet long by twenty-five feet beam, and crowded with passengers. The first-class accommodation consisted of a stuffy cabin in which I could barely stand upright. It measured exactly twenty feet in length by fifteen wide, and, as we numbered over a dozen, and the thermometer varied throughout from 80° to 95° Fahr., the journey can scarcely be described as enjoyable. One could scarcely move, night or day, without touching somebody. Our party at starting included two ladies, but I was much relieved to see them disappear at the first station. One grew accustomed in time to even these cramped quarters, but the disgusting food was beyond anything I have ever experienced, or even pictured. One Elia, an oleaginous individual in greasy black broadcloth, whose shirt, like everything else about him, was ingrained with the dirt of ages, controlled the cooking arrangements and waited at table, but had the *cuisine* excelled that of the Savoy Restaurant itself, the presence of Elia would certainly have deterred me from touching a morsel. Brackish water was the only drink obtainable, but as Philimónoff had brought a case of Crimean claret, and there was plenty of ice to be had at the stations, we fared well enough in this respect. Fish, eggs, and vegetables were also plentiful, and on these the *Paroutchik** and I subsisted, eating our meals on the tiny deck, till we arrived at Stretynsk.

We passed forty-two stations during the journey, and stopped at perhaps half that number. The arrival of the steamer was invariably the signal for a general assemblage of the

---

* Lieutenant.

villagers at the *Pristain*, which, on Sundays and holidays, presented a gay and picturesque appearance. The feminine element is distinctly more attractive on the Upper and on the Lower Amour, and at one of the larger stations, Tchernayeff, there were many pretty faces in the crowd — a rare occurrence in Eastern Siberia. These rustic maidens were apparently not troubled with diffidence. The day being very warm, a group of them moved away to a spot not a hundred yards from the steamer, and calmly proceeded to undress and bathe in the river regardless of onlookers. But no one seemed to pay any attention, so this is perhaps the custom of the country.

The main street of Tchernayeff was swarming with soldiers, many of whom had apparently paid more than one visit to the village *Traktir*,* kept by a villainous-looking old Jew with corkscrew ringlets. The men belonged to a regiment of Amour Cossacks, and were

---

* Public-house.

on their way to Nikolsk,* near Vladivostok. They were descending the Amour on rafts. Forty or fifty of the latter were moored to the bank just above the station, and a number of wiry-looking ponies belonging to the regiment were picketed in a meadow hard by. The rafts were built of rough-hewn logs, with a rough shed at either end for the accommodation of men and horses, those occupied by officers being distinguished by a white flag and better dwelling-places. Some of the latter were really luxuriously furnished, and embellished with lace window curtains, and flower-boxes. This economical mode of moving troops has only lately been adopted in Siberia. Regiments were formerly moved by steamer, but the present system has been found quite as effectual, especially as time is generally of no object. The expenses are practically nil, the current supplying the motive power and the rafts being constructed by the men themselves.

* See Chapter VII.

We reached Albazin on the following day, a town of some importance in former times, having been the seat of many hard-fought battles. Traces of old fortifications may still be seen, and old arms, pottery, etc., are occasionally brought to light by those (but they are few) who care to look for them. Albazin was once noted for its sables, which are, however, seldom found now in its vicinity. We stayed here for the night, and the thermometer fell 30° Fahr. after sunset, which enabled me to obtain a good night's rest, a luxury unobtainable since leaving Blagovieshtchensk, on account of the swarms of mosquitoes and stifling heat. The sudden fall of temperature was explained next day, when I saw that snow still lay deep in the valleys adjoining the river.

On the 21st of July, about midday, we entered the swift and dangerous Shilka River that sometimes, after heavy rains, rushes into the Amour with the force of a mountain torrent. The scenery here surpassed anything we had as yet seen. Precipitous mountains surround the river on every side, and at times seemed to landlock us completely. In places huge crags of granite, that looked as if a child could dislodge them, towered immediately overhead, and signs of avalanches were constantly visible in the shape of huge masses of rock, earth, and fir-trees which had fallen and lay partially submerged on either side of the swift-flowing stream. Our progress was now much slower, and at times the tiny tug could hardly make any perceptible headway against the current, which runs like a mill-race. The difficulty of navigation was evident, for we passed two steamers aground (one a total wreck) between the junction of the Shilka and Amour and Stretynsk. The latter was reached at midday on the 24th of June, after a journey of rather more than three weeks from the sea at Vladivostok.

CHAPTER XI.

THE SILVER MINES OF NERTCHINSK.

Part I.—GORNI-ZERENTUI.

STRETYNSK, although considerably smaller than either Khabarovsk or Blagovieshtchensk, is neatly laid out, and presents, from the river, an imposing appearance which is not so rudely dispelled as usual, in Siberia, on closer acquaintance. There are one or two fine buildings and several good shops in the principal street, which runs parallel to the river, and notably a very fair hotel rejoicing in the name of the "Vauxhall," which is kept by a Polish political exile who served four years in the mines. Mine host, Monsieur Mikouline, had now entirely forgotten his unpleasant experiences at Nertchinsk, and, judging from his charges, must have been rapidly amassing a fortune. This is apparently not unusual in these parts, for another ex-(criminal) convict, Monsieur L——, whose palatial residence is the sight of the place, has an income of £8,000 per annum. Madame L—— was pointed out to me, in a faultless *toilette*, driving up and down the muddy main street in a carriage and pair that would not have looked amiss in the Bois de Boulogne; but I found on inquiry that her husband was absent from home and undergoing a sentence of six months' imprisonment for a swindling transaction. This fact, however, did not seem in any way to detract from this gentleman's social position in the eyes of the inhabitants of Stretynsk.

Having visited the "Ispravnik" and arranged to start for the mines at five o'clock the following morning, Philimónoff and I adjourned to the "Vauxhall," and partook of a parting meal in a pretty vine-trellised balcony overhanging the river. Hearing that I had an autograph letter from the Governor-General,

Monsieur Mikouline had excelled himself, and provided a delicious dinner consisting of *Akroshka*,* salmon trout, and a roast capon, which, washed down with well-iced Pommery (price thirty shillings a bottle), was a pleasant change after the tasteless garbage on board the barge. Coffee and liqueurs protracted this pleasant repast until sunset, when my friend set out on a long drive of over 1,500 miles to Tomsk, and I retired to rest on a clean and comfortable sofa. Here, however, as in most Siberian cities, the night watchmen render night hideous with the clinking of metal, and it was long before I closed my eyes. When I awoke it was past eight o'clock, but the hotel was still wrapped in silence, nor was there a sign of the vehicle faithfully promised by the "Ispravnik"; while, to make matters worse, the sky was of a dull leaden hue, and the rain pouring down in torrents. The hotel was apparently deserted, and having shouted

---

* Iced soup.

in vain for the shock-headed lad who performed the twofold duties of waiter and housemaid, I set out on foot through the slush and driving rain for the "Ispravnik's" house, and was met half-way by the *telega*, a ramshackle conveyance even more dilapidated than the one that had brought me to Boussè. During my absence Monsieur Mikouline had arisen from his slumbers and prepared breakfast, but there was no time to be lost, if we did not wish to spend the night upon the road, so hastily swallowing a couple of glasses of scalding tea, I climbed into the cart and we galloped away through the mud, which, ere we had covered half a mile, gave me the appearance of having been dragged through a sea of mire.

My first destination was the village of Gorni-Zerentui, about 260 versts distant, where the largest prison in the Nertchinsk mining district is situated. This establishment is used only for criminal convicts, all political offenders being confined at Akatui, 200 versts further west. It may here be well to give the reader a brief sketch of the journey which convicts exiled by land from Europe must accomplish before reaching the mines of the Trans-Baikal.

An average of 17,000 exiles per annum have left European Russia within the past fifteen years for Siberia, which contains (exclusive of Sakhalin) about 230 prisons. Only a very small proportion (perhaps four per cent.) of the exiles belong to the upper classes, and quite two-thirds are utterly illiterate. Neither are they all felons in a true sense of the word, since the *Mir*, or village parliament, has the power of punishing unruly members of society for general misconduct, such as idleness and insobriety, and these number perhaps thirty per cent. of the total. It is, perhaps, not generally known that the number of free emigrants to Siberia far exceeds that of the enforced exiles, and is annually increasing. The voluntary settlers who passed through the Government of Tobolsk in 1885 numbered only 9,600; but these figures had increased in 1891 to 60,000, and rose the following year to nearly 100,000. Siberia is generally becoming the *El Dorado* of the Russian peasant. It is a case of Australia over again.

About two-thirds of the prisons I have mentioned are *étapes*, or resting-places, stationed along the great post road that leads to the Pacific. Thirty years ago, exiles were compelled to walk every step of the way from Moscow to the mines. They now travel by rail and river to Tomsk, accomplishing at least half the journey under much more favourable circumstances. At Tomsk, only, the actual march eastward commences, gangs being formed of from three to four hundred men, women, and children. The escort usually consists of one soldier to every twenty prisoners, and from twenty to thirty *telegas* accompanying each convoy for the use of the sick and for transport of baggage. Progression is from eighteen to twenty miles a day, marching two days and resting one. Unlike in the prisons, there is, on the road, no diet scale, each convict receiving a fixed sum daily with which he may buy anything he pleases, excepting alcohol. Smoking is not only permitted, but even encouraged in the *étapes*, which are one-storeyed wooden buildings with three public cells, one of which is set apart for women. The reader has probably heard something about these *étapes*; perhaps not much to their credit. Personally speaking, I have seen good ones and also very bad ones, but I am glad to say that the latter are now in the minority—at any rate, in Western Siberia.

It is only, then, at Tomsk that the march commences along the great Siberian post road, which, by the way, is little better than a mere track cut by caravan traffic. A man sentenced, for instance, to penal servitude at the mines, travels on foot to Irkoutsk (the capital of Eastern Siberia), a journey of about two months. A week beyond Irkoutsk, he crosses Lake Baikal (a huge sheet of water more than sixty times the area of the Lake of Geneva) in a wooden hulk towed by a steamer. Landing on the eastern shore he resumes his march through a wild and mountainous region, and three or four weeks later (according to the state of the roads) reaches his destination, after a journey from European Russia of ten to fifteen months, which once took two years, at least, to accomplish.

The silver mines of Nertchinsk, near the Chinese frontier, are now the only ones in Siberia where convict labour is employed. There are seven prisons, containing altogether from 3,000 to 4,000 prisoners, and about a dozen mines scattered over a district nearly 200 miles long by 100 broad. *The mines are silver mines.* It is probably unnecessary to remind the reader that quicksilver is not (and never has been) worked in Siberia, and that reports of convicts slowly rotting to death underground have been conclusively proved to be absolutely untrue. The mines of Nertchinsk were first worked in 1760 by serfs. It was only after the emancipation of the latter that prisoners were employed. All minerals found are the property of the Tsar.

We pulled up for the night at the station of Shalopougina, having travelled seventy-two versts, which, considering the shocking state of the road, was not bad work. The rain had never ceased for an instant, and as a dense white mist obscured objects only a few yards distant, the drive was not only comfortless, but so uninteresting that I agreed to the Yemstchik's proposal to halt at Shalopougina, instead of Undinsky-Kavikotchi, twenty versts further on. It was indeed a relief to enter a warm, brightly-lit room after that cheerless journey. My clothes clung to me like a bathing-dress, and even the contents of my bag were saturated by the pitiless rain. But several glasses of tea and a roaring fire soon mended matters, and after a hearty supper prepared by the rosy-cheeked postmistress, I lay down on the floor near the stove and soon forgot the miseries of the day. The incessant jolting of the past twelve hours had rendered me rather wakeful than otherwise, and day was dawning before I fell asleep. There is no weirder place in the world than the interior of a Siberian post house at night-time, when the inmates have retired to rest, leaving the solitary traveller to himself in the lonely guest-room. This is not so in Western regions, where the roads are thronged and passenger traffic keeps the Yemstchiks busy throughout the night, but east of Lake Baikal voyagers are scarce, especially after dark. By nine o'clock the lights are extinguished and a dead stillness reigns, broken only, as it was to-night, by mournful gusts of wind, the pattering of rain, and the squeaks and scratchings of the rats who, emboldened by the darkness, gradually emerge from the walls and flooring in unpleasantly large numbers. Amid such surroundings seconds become minutes and minutes hours, and the cry of a fractious infant or even an alarm of fire would be hailed with positive relief. Occasionally, but very rarely in these parts, a faint jingle of bells is heard, gradually increasing in volume till they clash loudly by the window and die away again in a wilderness of lonely moorland or dark pine forest. This was to me the most disquieting sound of all, for, although I cannot assign a reason, the sound of collar-bells at night has always (in Siberia) impressed me with a vague sense of approaching danger. The fact that the forests swarm with runaway convicts may have something to do with this, although I fancy the feeling was first engendered in me years ago by Sir Henry Irving in his terribly realistic rendering of the old Burgomaster, "Mathias," at the Lyceum Theatre.

A flood of brilliant sunshine was streaming through the fly-blown windows when I awoke, and a glance at the cloudless blue sky assured me that fine weather had set in, at least for the day. The air felt cool and fresh after the rain as we drove out of the village, and glorious scenery amply atoned for the discomfort of yesterday. The distant mountains, wide stretches of thyme-scented moorland, pine forests carpeted with fern and wild flowers, and pretty villages dotted over the smiling landscape, quite justify the name of "Siberian

Switzerland" that has been given to this district. Halting at midday at Undinsky-Kavikotchi (the villages here often contain more letters in their names than inhabitants) I reached Staina at sunset. We were now only sixty odd versts from our destination, and the post house being a clean one, I halted for the night—to my subsequent regret, for the Postmaster was a character, and never ceased chattering from the moment the *troika* was unharnessed until my departure next morning. The lines :

> I do not tremble when I meet
> The stoutest of my foes,
> But Heaven defend me from the friend
> Who never—never—goes !

well apply to mine host at Staina. The post house was surrounded by a well-kept flower and vegetable garden, and this I was at once led off to inspect. The stables followed, when I was informed that at Staina a cow fetches £3 and a horse £5. My friend's wife and offspring were then mustered for my inspection, but I was afterwards hurried back into the yard, for the pigs and poultry had been overlooked. Nor was the privacy of the guest-room a protection from this erratic being. The evening meal was served, and this he suggested sharing, pleasantly remarking that I must feel lonely. The man was absolutely irrepressible, so I resigned myself to circumstances and gave him a cigarette, which only increased his garrulity. His thirst for information about Europe was insatiable, but although he asked twenty questions in as many minutes, a reply was never paused for. My talkative host was still there when towards midnight I fell back on my furs exhausted, but, happening to awake a couple of hours later, I heard him still muttering in his sleep. What a terrible infirmity!

The approach to the famous mines, so often quoted in sensational literature, is anything but awe-inspiring. Gorni-Zerentui is a pretty village surrounded by undulating hills of rich pasture land. As I neared it, on that bright summer's day, very little stretch of imagination would have sufficed to fancy one's self in far-away England on the Wiltshire or Sussex downs, the white verst posts scattered across the grassy plain being quaintly suggestive of a racecourse, even in this remote corner of Asia—twenty miles from the Chinese frontier. The huge prison stands some distance away from the settlement, and its whitewashed walls form a prominent feature in the landscape. Clustered around it are the houses of the Governor and prison officials. My Yemstchik presently drew up in front of the former.

A stout, pleasant-featured, middle-aged man in white linen tunic and gold shoulder-straps, rose from a wicker chair by the porch and advanced to greet me. This was Monsieur Tomiline, the Governor, who had been apprised of my arrival by telegram from Stretynsk. I followed my host into the luxurious apartment replete with every European comfort that formed his *cabinet de travail*, and we partook of a *Zakouska* before adjourning to dinner, which was laid in an adjoining room. Monsieur Tomiline spoke only a few words of French, and I therefore noticed with some surprise, that his bookshelves contained nothing but works in that language, while back numbers of the *Figaro*, *Gil Blas*, and *La Vie Parisienne* were piled up in every available corner. It then transpired that Madame Tomiline, who had lately returned for a time to St. Petersburg, was an admirable French scholar. For this (not having seen a book for many weeks) I had reason to be thankful, and I revelled, after retiring to rest that night, in the works of Bourget, Zola, and Guy de Maupassant to my heart's content.

Early next morning I visited the prison accompanied by the Governor. It is the best penal establishment, from every point of view, that I have ever seen in Siberia. The building (which cost over 160,000 roubles, and is not even yet completed) is of whitewashed brick, and stands in a spacious yard surrounded by a brick wall eighteen feet high. The roof is of zinc and painted a dull red, which somewhat enlivens the gloomy appearance usually presented by a house of detention. Three smaller buildings, the hospital, bath, and laundry, are situated near each other on the northern side of the main building. Outside, at every corner of the wall, are sentry-boxes, where soldiers are stationed night and day with loaded rifles and revolvers.

As to the interior of the prison, if the reader has ever visited an English county jail, he has seen Gorni-Zerentui, for it is built on exactly the same model. The prison is two-storeyed, the principal hall measuring 168 feet by 22 feet, and 45 feet high. Eight large "Kameras" (four on each storey) are approached by light iron ladders and balconies, the latter completely surrounding the hall. I visited every "Kamera" and found them light, well ventilated, and by no means overcrowded. Large barred windows afforded a view of the surrounding country on every side. In summer, for coolness' sake, iron gratings are substituted for wooden doors. The sleeping and sanitary arrangements are much the same as at Alexandrovsky-Post, and the Governor informed me that, here only, every "Kamera" is continually overlooked at night by a warder who is relieved every two hours. Each ward is also fitted with an electric bell which renders bullying, that curse of Siberian prison life, an impossibility.

The prison contained 429 men, of whom only ninety-one were out at work in the mine about two miles distant. The question of labour is one of the chief difficulties with which the Siberian authorities have to contend. Many of the "Kameras" at Gorni-Zerentui were filled with men idling listlessly about, who would only too gladly have turned to work of any kind to lighten their weary hours of captivity. Perhaps ten per cent. or more of those left in prison were employed at tailoring and shoe-making, certainly not more. The Governor told me (and I can quite believe it) that he sometimes punished men by depriving them of their day's work outside the prison walls.

We then set out for the orphanage, adjoining the prison. As we passed through the gateway a gang of convicts entered, and I noticed that some of the men carried nosegays of wild flowers gathered on their way back from the shaft. These they took into the building, which fact occasioned me some surprise. "You are looking at the flowers," said Tomiline, half apologetically. "I know it is not in order. They would not permit such an *enfantillage* in England, but the flowers can do no harm, and give the poor fellows pleasure, so I do not interfere."

A group of women were standing in the road, some with babies in their arms, as we emerged from the prison gateway. One of them approached us and handed the Governor a paper, which he proceeded to read. I could see disappointment in the woman's face when it was handed back to her, and asked the reason.

"That is the wife of a man who arrived

with the last gang," said Tomiline. "You are probably aware that wives are permitted to accompany their husbands out here, and that, after a term in prison, the latter are liberated. These poor souls, many of whom come here, expect that their husbands will be liberated at once. This is of course impossible."

"How long must these women wait," I asked, "and how do they live in the meantime?"

"It all depends on the crime. Some men remain in prison only six months—others from one to five years; seldom longer."

"But how do their wives and families exist meanwhile?"

"That is our great difficulty," replied Tomiline. "Some are employed as domestic servants in the village by the freed political exiles, but, as you may imagine, the majority can find no employment. An allowance of thirty-six pounds of bread per month is provided to each by the Government, but few have the courage to await their husbands' freedom for more than a couple of years. They drift away to Irkoutsk, or some other city, and I fear that many go to the bad. There is their village," added the Governor, pointing to a collection of rather dilapidated-looking huts about a verst equidistant from the prison and village. "It contains over 200 women and children at present, and the number will probably increase before the end of the transportation season. *Que voulez-vous?*" added my friend, with a shrug of the shoulders. "We do it for the best, and in many cases, though by no means always, the plan succeeds."

"And the wives of political exiles?" I asked.

"There are about a dozen in the village," was his reply. "Their husbands are, as you know, never confined here, but at Akatui. Their wives have good houses at either place, and live exactly as they would in Russia, according to their means. Most of them seem to be well supplied with money."

The orphanage at Gorni-Zerentui consists of two substantial wooden buildings containing school-room, dormitories, and quarters for the matron and her assistant, and a number of smaller buildings, stables, workshops, etc., enclosing a large playground. This institution was built almost entirely by private subscriptions, and Madame Narishkine, a lady-in-waiting of the Dowager Empress, was the original promoter of the scheme. It contained twenty boys and twenty-eight girls, whose ages varied from four to fourteen years. Many of the children had parents either in prison or living in the village, so that the term orphanage is perhaps a misnomer. We were received by the matron, a quiet, ladylike person, whose sitting-room was a perfect wealth of wild flowers, brought in from the fields by the children. Mademoiselle R—— was assisted by her niece, who had, of her own free will, abandoned a life of civilisation and gaiety for existence in these dreary wilds. Both these ladies were well-born, and had moved in good society in St. Petersburg, and a photograph of a group of children, which I took in the playground, speaks for itself as to the comfort and well-being of the poor little waifs committed to their care.

Part II.—THE POLITICAL PRISON OF AKATUI.

THERE is no regular post road between Gorni-Zerentui and Akatui, a distance of 200 versts. The latter is situated in a lonely valley, and lies far away from the beaten track, the nearest settlement to it being Alexandrovsky-Zavod. This, which now contains 1,500 inhabitants, was once the principal penal settlement of Nertchinsk (the word "Zavod" signifying "Works"), but of late years the mines in its vicinity have been abandoned, and the exiles distributed among the seven penal establishments scattered over the district.

Bidding adieu to my kind host, I set out on the morning of the third day after my arrival, for Akatui. Glorious sunshine and pure exhilarating air made the journey, which lay over a succession of rolling downs, very enjoyable. I passed the first night at a comfortable rest house provided by the Government for prison officials while travelling, and, passing

GOVERNOR'S HOUSE, BARRACKS, AND PART OF OLD PRISON, AKATUI.
The only place in Siberia where *political* convicts are now sent to hard labour in the mines.

through the large straggling village of Alexandrovsky-Zavod the next day at noon, approached my destination towards evening.

Akatui is a natural prison in the midst of precipitous mountains which, upon entering the desolate valley, seem to close upon one like a trap. As I drove through the village at dusk the squalid houses seemed almost deserted. Here and there a light glimmered, darkened for an instant as the jingle of the collar-bells brought some startled inmate to the window, but although barely sunset, most of the inmates, chiefly freed political exiles, had retired to rest. The prison stands just outside the village. There is an air of gloom and severity about the place, very different to that I have noticed in most Siberian jails. Armed warders meet one at every turn, and the very hill-tops bristle with sentries. Although nearly every prison throughout Siberia has its yearly average of convicts "missing," no one has ever yet escaped from Akatui, nor, judging from appearances, ever will, for the strictest military discipline prevails, and the slightest infringement of rules by either prisoners or warders is punished with an iron hand. I have already explained that, although occasionally banished to remote places within the Arctic Circle, political prisoners *condemned to penal servitude* in Siberia are sent here, and here only. State prisoners were formerly confined at the gold mines of Kará, a short distance from here, where they were kept quite apart from ordinary criminals. Kará has now been entirely abolished, and all its inmates transferred to Akatui, where no distinction whatever is made. Political exiles do the same work, eat the same food, and wear the same clothes as common felons, and sleep in the public "Kamera" side by side with the first murderer, thief, or vagabond that chance may bring. For this reason some of the exiles here consider themselves worse off than at Kará State Prison, but others assured me that they preferred even promiscuous herding with the vilest criminals to the maddening silence of solitary confinement. As regards natural surroundings the change is hardly for the better, for one of the very few travellers who have visited Akatui writes: "If there is in Siberia a more lonely, a more cheerless, a more God-forsaken place than Kará, it is the snowy, secluded valley of Akatui," and I can quite believe it.

I arrived at Akatui thoroughly exhausted and done up. Want of food, the merciless jolting over 200 versts of ground, and exposure to a blazing sun had brought on nausea and a splitting headache, which, coupled with feverish symptoms, predicted a longer stay here than I had bargained for. The prospect of being laid up for an indefinite period at the mines occurred to me with unpleasant reality, as I staggered rather than walked into the house of the Governor, Colonel Archangelski. The Colonel received me with true Russian hospitality, and insisted on my at once retiring to rest in his bed (the only one in the house), where, after a strong dose of quinine, I fell into a dreamless sleep that lasted twelve hours, awaking with every trace of fever vanished, but still so weak and stiff that one leg would scarcely move before the other. My host was kindness itself, and I fancy few men of my acquaintance would willingly sleep on bare boards to oblige a friend, much less a stranger.

Archangelski's house was of wood, sur-

THE GOVERNOR AND PRISON WARDERS, AKATUI PRISON.

rounded by a large flower and vegetable garden, and commanded a fine view of the valley from end to end. To the right of it was a guard house, occupied by the Assistant Governor, a captain of Cossacks, and his two hundred men. Exactly opposite this is the prison, a comparatively new wooden building, which we visited on the first occasion at noon, just before the dinner hour. *Déjeuner* was served before we set out, by a pleasant-looking, neatly-dressed waiting maid of about thirty—a very unusual occurrence in Siberia, where men-servants are usually employed. Inquiry elicited the fact that "Marya" was an ex-convict, sent for life to Siberia for cleaving her husband's skull open with a hatchet while he slept. "We are all waited on by convicts," said Archangelski, half apologetically. "But I always employ assassins. They make far better servants than thieves. My 'Yemstchik' is also a murderer."

The Akatui prison is enclosed and entirely concealed from the outside world by a brick wall twenty feet in height, with a *chevaux-*

de-frise, and surrounded night and day by armed sentries. An oaken door several inches thick and heavily clamped with iron was unbarred by a warder, and swung back with a crash behind us as we entered the court-yard. The day being Sunday, no work of any kind was going on. The heat was tropical, and we found many convicts in the yard lounging listlessly about or sitting in the scanty shade thrown by the building. About one third wore irons,* and the clanking of chains was incessant. The prison itself is comparatively small, containing only eight "Kameras." Two smaller buildings, the infirmary and kitchen, stand right and left of the entrance.

We first visited the "Kameras," which were nearly empty, most of their occupants having, for the sake of coolness, sought the yard. The prison contained in all 108, but could easily have held twice that number. I found the cells scrupulously clean; many of them

---

* See Appendix H.

with walls and floors decorated with pine boughs, the scent of which, mingled with cigarette smoke, pervaded the place. Nearly every "Kamera" contained a few bookshelves, the property of the State prisoners, and here, as at Gorni-Zerentui, some of the tin drinking mugs contained bunches of wild flowers. The sleeping platforms could be folded back during the daytime, and each "Kamera" was lit by a large barred window, made so as to open or shut at the discretion of the inmates. Mattresses and pillows were rolled up with care and neatness, the sleeping places of political exiles being easily distinguishable by the toilet requisites, books, and writing materials kept on the shelves immediately overhead.

I fancy many people imagine that in the case of political offenders, exile to Siberia must mean banishment *for ever*. They are apt to overlook the fact that there are many grades of political exile, from the lifelong imprisonment at the mines, to a couple of months just over the Asiatic frontier. Another popular fallacy is that political offenders are kept to hard labour to the bitter end of their sentence—till death puts an end to their misery. This, is no doubt so occasionally, but only in very serious cases, the majority being released after a term of years (according to the gravity of their offence), and permitted to live (under police supervision only) in the town or village to which they are assigned.

Of the 108 convicts at Akatui twenty-seven were politicals, three of whom were in chains. A pair of them is now in my possession; they weigh about seven pounds, and are riveted round the ankles and secured by a leather strap to the waist. These irons are invariably removed from all prisoners before work in the mines, which is carried on throughout the year. Save that less work is done, the conditions of labour are much the same as in our English mines. In summer the men rise at five a.m., and, after a meal of porridge and black bread, march to the shaft, a mile distant. At noon they return to the prison for dinner, which consists of soup, and, three times a week, meat and kvas. By two o'clock they are in the mines again and work on till seven p.m., when they return to the prison and partake of gruel, black bread, and tea. Smoking is universal (excepting underground), and lights are put out at nine p.m. In winter time the working hours are from seven a.m. to four p.m., and on Sundays and saints' days no work of any kind is done, either in prison or out of it. As my sole object in coming to 'Akatui was to ascertain the condition of the political exiles confined there (if possible from their own lips), I wasted no time over technical details, and Colonel Archangelski promptly fell in with my suggestion that we should visit them without delay. I then found that, although the latter are compelled at night to share the public cells with common felons, a room in the prison is set apart for their use in the daytime where they may write, read, or receive (once a week) the friends who have accompanied them into exile and live in the adjacent village.

"We will first visit the invalids," said the Governor, leading the way to the hospital, which, in addition to a light, roomy, well-ventilated ward, contained a consulting room, a dispensary, and four double-bedded rooms. Entering one of the latter we found two exiles, one a clean-shaven, under-sized man about thirty years old, and the other a tall, good-looking fellow, with a long fair beard, who towered over his companion, and whose appearance was not unprepossessing, even in the hideous gray frieze prison garb that hung so loosely and grotesquely on his companion's diminutive frame. Prison clothes in Siberia are apparently made exclusively for men six feet high, and no allowance is made for size. The floor was bare, and the sole furniture two wooden chairs, a small table by the window with books and writing materials, and two iron bedsteads with sheets and pillows ranged foot to foot along one side of the whitewashed wall.

Both men rose as we entered, and the

smaller of the two approached us and (in excellent French) politely wished me good-day. The Governor (who had uncovered when he entered the apartment) then left me, promising to return in half an hour, thereby enabling me to converse on any subject as freely as I could wish.

I was then given one of the two chairs, Göttze, the Jewish exile, taking the other, while Vraginsky, his comrade, remained standing. The latter was a somewhat shy, reserved man, and Göttze acted as spokesman throughout. We spoke in French, although Göttze was acquainted with English. "No," he said, in answer to my first and important question, "no, we cannot complain of actual ill-treatment, but this is an awful place. I have thought at times that I should lose my reason, but, thank God, I have grown out of that. Kará was bad enough, but there, at any rate, there was a certain amount of privacy. Here, when not in hospital, we are indiscriminately herded with the vilest and most degraded criminals, and the nights," he added with a shudder, "are sometimes too horrible for description."

Göttze then told me that he had been sent to the mines for life for participation in the Yakoutsk revolt (which resulted in the death of many Guards and exiles) in 1889, while Vraginsky was undergoing a sentence of twenty years' penal servitude for the same offence. Both men had been here eight years. The wife of Göttze was living in Akatui, and was permitted to visit her husband once a week, while Vraginsky's late mistress, Paulina Perli, lived with Madame Göttze and enjoyed the same privileges.

Notwithstanding their long estrangement from the world, both Göttze and Vraginsky displayed a knowledge of current events that greatly astonished me. On my mentioning, for instance, that I occasionally corresponded from Siberia with the *Pall Mall Gazette*, Vraginsky remarked: "Stead has nothing to do with that now, has he?" and before I could reply Göttze had answered: "No, no. It belongs to Waldorf Astor, the American millionaire. Stead now has the *Review of Reviews*. I used to receive it at Yakoutsk," he added sadly, "but I may not have it now."

"And yet you are allowed certain works," said I, taking up a volume haphazard from the table. It was the Socialist leader, Hyndman's "Crises of the Nineteenth Century,"* in English. Göttze looked at Vraginsky, and both smiled at my astonishment.

"That has slipped in by mistake," explained the former. "The Governor does not speak your language, nor, indeed, does any one here, except two or three among *us*. That is a grand work. I am translating it into Russian, but I fear it will never be published. It is too advanced for Russia," he added, with a heavy sigh.

"Then you may receive as many books as your friends care to send you?" I asked.

---

* "Commercial Crises of the Nineteenth Century." By H. M. Hyndman. Swan, Sonnenschein, & Co., London.

"Yes. But before they reach us, all are read by Archangelski, who does not often confiscate them. There is no fault to find with him. He is a just man."

"For a Russian official!" chimed in Vraginsky, which created a general laugh.

"And how often do you send and receive letters?"

"Once a month. These are also read by Archangelski before despatch or delivery."

We then conversed on general topics, and Göttze's familiarity with recent Socialistic and other events in Europe convinced me that, jealously guarded as they are, the Akatui politicals manage to communicate (and pretty frequently) with the outside world.

Half an hour had scarcely elapsed when the Governor returned. I then took leave of my friends, but did not depart without some difficulty. It was truly pathetic to see the eagerness with which the poor fellows started a new subject of conversation whenever I made a movement to go, and the efforts made by Göttze to prolong an interview, the like of which might not occur again for many weary years.

The cell adjoining this was identically similar to the one we had just left, but contained only one occupant, a stout, florid, middle-aged man, with spectacles and thin reddish-gray hair. He was writing as we entered, but rose, gave us a stiff bow and reseated himself, and resumed his occupation without even glancing again in our direction. A look from Archangelski warned me not to speak, and having received a curt negative as to whether there were any complaints, the Governor signalled me to follow him out of the cell. This, he whispered, was Slavinsky, one of the cleverest and most dangerous revolutionists in Russia.

Slavinsky's history was a remarkable one, as exemplifying the irony of fate. He had only recently arrived at Akatui, having originally been arrested at Berlin for a very trivial political offence, for which he would probably have undergone imprisonment for only a few weeks. By the advice, however, of an over-zealous German lawyer, he claimed exemption on the ground of his Russian nationality, and was (much against his wish) promptly extradited to St. Petersburg. A plot, in which he was implicated, had only recently been discovered in that city, and Slavinsky was again arraigned on the charge that finally led to his deportation for life to the mines of Siberia.

Before visiting the politicals in the main building, I walked through the hospital ward, which contained fifty beds, nearly half of which were occupied, mostly by patients suffering from the prevailing epidemic, influenza, which was raging throughout the district. Although that scourge of prison life, typhus, and other infectious diseases, are rare here, Akatui cannot be called a healthy locality, for notwithstanding that it is situated over 3,000 feet above sea-level, it is marshy and malarious. The severity of its climate in winter, which lasts from August to May, is only equalled by the intense heat of the brief summer, when the thermometer often registers 95° Fahr. in the shade at midday, notwithstanding that the soil is always frozen at a depth of twenty-eight inches. The latter circumstance may perhaps account for the dense white mists that, during my visit, enshrouded the place towards sunset; and I generally returned from an evening stroll with my clothes wringing wet. It did not, therefore, surprise me to find that the prevailing complaints are of a pulmonary and rheumatic nature. Other diseases are rare. A man of robust constitution would probably suffer little from the climatic influences, which, to one of weaker build, would no doubt, sooner or later, prove fatal.

Re-entering the prison we visited a room which is, as I have already said, kept apart for the use of political exiles during the daytime. It contained three exiles, all clad in convict dress. The apartment was whitewashed, bare and carpetless, with two large barred windows looking on to the prison yard.

A number of books, chiefly scientific works, were on a small table, and a printing-press stood in a corner. All the men rose as we entered, and I noticed that one, who looked almost a boy, wore leg fetters, which he vainly tried to conceal behind a chair. This was Khotchurikin, undergoing a life sentence for the attempted assassination of General Paltarovski, the Governor of Kazan. The others were Minor and Ouflandt. The first named, a tall, dark man, about thirty years old, smiled pleasantly when I addressed him in English, but looked weak and ill, and leaned for support against the wall. Minor is here for life, but the Governor told me that a few months have considerably aged him. He is of good family, and has taken high honours at Yardslav University. His brother is a professor of Moscow University, and was a pupil of the famous Charcot. Minor's refined appearance and manner contrasted strangely with his poor surroundings — the barred windows, clanking chains, and crowd of villainous faces gathered at the open doorway. Ouflandt was a medical student, with a sentence of twenty years. He had been here only a year, and had already learnt to speak and write the English language very fairly.

Here, as before, the Governor left me for a considerable time, and I was eagerly questioned for news from the outer world, which I was only too glad to be able to give to the best of my ability. Minor told me that as regards food and treatment there was little to complain about, but like all the other prisoners, he complained bitterly of being compelled to share a public ward with the criminal convicts. Work in the mines, he said, was not unduly severe, although the rotten ladders leading down some of the shafts had caused several accidents. A man had been killed from this cause only a week before my arrival. This exile also informed me that a "manifesto" had been issued on the occasion of the Tsarevitch's journey through Siberia, reducing the life sentences of political convicts at Akatui to twenty years, and minor sentences in proportion. This commutation, however, did not apply to either Slavinsky or Khotchurikin, neither of whom will ever leave Akatui.

I left the prison at dusk to return to the Governor's house, where I found my host and the Commander of the Cossack Guard, Lieutenant Estousheffsky, immersed in the contents of a mail-bag that had just arrived from Nertchinsk. A pile of over fifty unopened letters lay between them, to say nothing of a dozen or more large volumes which had arrived from Europe for the political exiles. Both these and the letters would have to be carefully examined before delivery, and the work was not completed till late the following day. Two, only, of the books were confiscated. Among those distributed to their owners, I noticed the following:

"Simulatsia Loushevnik Boliezni," by Dr. Govsieff. Kharkoff, 1894.

"Varajdenia" by Max Nordau. Translation from the German. St. Petersburg, 1894.

"Practica Vienski Klinik," by Dr. Theodor Wiethe. St. Petersburg, 1893. (A pocket manual of Medicine.)

COLONEL ARCHANGELSKI.

A mail was also leaving, and contained a letter from Ouflandt to his mother. "An Englishman," he said, "has visited us to-day.

I should like to have had a long talk with him. It will be interesting to see what he writes about us. Try and send me the newspaper." This letter was sent to its destination without erasure of any kind.

I devoted the next morning to an inspection of the mine. There are three shafts at Akatui, situated about a mile from the prison. They are called the "Stolna," "Leuft Loch," and "Aninskaya," and are distant from each other only a few hundred yards. The "Stolna," which is now the only one in operation, is driven horizontally through the side of a hill to a distance of about 150 yards. I walked to the furthest extremity, along a gallery six feet high by four feet broad, supported at every fifteen feet by strong timbers. A tramway runs the entire length. About forty men were at work in the mine, which seemed engineered and ventilated according to the most modern ideas, and with due regard to the safety of the miners. The shafts in operation in the Nertchinsk district are seven in number, and vary from 50 to 250 feet deep. Kadaya is the oldest, having been established over 100 years. The disused shafts at Akatui were both perpendicular, and a glance into the gloomy depths of the deserted "Aninskaya" soon convinced me of the truth of Minor's statement, for although work here had only lately been abandoned, many of the ladder rungs were missing, and even the first platform was a frail, rickety structure, in places completely rotted away. Women are now never, under any circumstances, sent below ground. A special prison, Pokorovsky (about twenty versts from here), is allotted to them, where they are put to work suitable to their sex. The mines of Nertchinsk can scarcely be called remunerative, for in 1893 the output of the entire district did not amount to one ton.

I paid the same evening a visit to the prison shortly after midnight. My request to be allowed to do so somewhat surprised the Governor, for it was made unexpectedly as we were retiring to rest. But he immediately assented, good-naturedly humouring what he called my *toquade*, and we set out forthwith. The night was close and stifling, and the windows of the dimly-lit "Kameras" thrown wide open, which enabled us to see into the wards unobserved, for a time, by the inmates. They were lying stretched out in all directions on the sleeping platforms. Some of them had divested themselves of the heavy gray prison cloak, and were pacing slowly up and down the wards in linen shirt and drawers. There was little stillness or rest about the place, for the clink of fetters was unceasing, and the majority of those lying down were tossing feverishly from side to side, moaning or cursing in their sleep. "Plokha,"* said Archangelski with a shrug of his shoulders, and I then saw that the walls and flooring were swarming with vermin. Akatui prison is only five years old, but scarcely a year after its completion these pests made their appearance, as they will do sooner

---

* Bugs.

or later in every Siberian dwelling, be its occupant peer or peasant. The "Kameras," on the other hand, were free from smell and not overcrowded, although I could readily understand Göttze's aversion to sharing night quarters with the villainous-looking wretches that, presently espying us outside, advanced to the window and made us beat a hasty retreat.

As we left the prison towards one a.m., the Governor directed the sentry by the entrance gate to blow the alarm whistle. This was instantly replied to by a deafening crash of rattles and gongs from all points of the compass, while far away the silent hills resounded with a volley of musketry. There has only been one (attempted) escape from here during the past twenty years, and in this case the fugitive was captured and brought back within twenty-four hours.

Leaving Akatui early the following morning, I reached Stretynsk on the evening of the second day after a drive of nearly 600 versts, or about 400 English miles. That political exiles at Akatui are humanely treated, and that (save in one respect) their life is made as tolerable as circumstances will permit, I can readily believe. Yet, notwithstanding that only the most dangerous are sent here, to compel such men as Minor, for instance, to associate closely and continually with the vilest criminals (when a "Kamera" for politicals could be easily set apart) seems to me not only cruel but unnecessary, and in direct opposition to the generally humane mode of treatment that I have found in other Siberian prisons.

CHAPTER XII.

THE LOWER AMOUR. KHABAROVSK—NIKOLAEFSK.

An account of my return from Stretynsk down the Amour River would probably weary the reader as much, if not more, than the actual journey did the writer, which is saying a good deal. Suffice it, then, to say that I reached Khabarovsk, after an uneventful voyage, on the morning of the 15th of July, and, the Governor-General being absent, at once applied to the Chief of Police for a paper authorising me to obtain horses without delay on the road from Boussè to Tchernigovka. A document of this kind is worth fifty ordinary *Padarojnas*,* but the official's reply was only con-

---

* A paper authorising travellers to use Government post horses.

sistent with the glorious uncertainty of Siberian travel. To reach Vladivostok by the way of Boussè was, he explained, at present quite impossible, for two reasons: one being that the country south of Boussè was entirely submerged for many miles; the other that, glanders having broken out at Shmakovka, the Governor-General had issued stringent orders that no horses but those carrying the mails should pass through the infected district. As I had quite made up my mind that ten days more would find me on board a comfortable steamer bound for Japan, this was, to say the least of it, disappointing. Retreat, however, was now completely cut off by my old route, and there was nothing for it but to proceed in the *Baron Korff* to Nikolaefsk, which entailed a *détour* of some 1,500 miles, with the off chance of being snowed up in that dreary northern settlement till the following spring—a cheerful prospect indeed! But experience has taught me the futility of quarrelling with fate (especially in Siberia), and I re-embarked on board the *Baron Korff* as cheerfully as circumstances would permit, and quite prepared for the worst. Towards evening of the same day I resumed my voyage, much to the surprise of the captain, from whom I had parted, ostensibly for good, in the morning.

I now had the boat to myself, nor was there much likelihood of any passengers embarking *en route*. The distance to Nikolaefsk is nearly 700 English miles, and although the *Baron Korff* was now towing a huge iron, heavily-laden barge, the swift current carried us along so rapidly that the captain expected to reach our destination in less than four days. As we left Khabarovsk a terrific thunderstorm burst over the town, accompanied by forked lightning and torrents of rain. The heat all day had been tropical, but the thermometer, which had stood at 96° in the shade, sank twenty degrees in less than a quarter of an hour, so sudden are the changes of temperature in these parts. A breeze then sprang up, which in a few hours increased to a stiff gale of wind. By midnight it was blowing a hurricane, and the *Baron Korff* was lying with two anchors out in a sea which, even in the English Channel, would have been accounted heavy, for this portion of the Amour is in places many miles wide. I have seldom passed a more wretched night. Sleep was out of the question, and having been twice pitched out of my berth, I lay on the floor for the remainder of the night, listening to the howling of the tempest, and dismally wondering whether I had only escaped drowning on the Upper, to find a watery grave in the Lower Amour. Towards daybreak the storm reached its height. The *Baron Korff* was now tugging at her anchors so violently that it seemed as if the cables must part, while every now and then a huge sea would break over the bows, sweeping the vessel from stem to stern, and flooding the cabins and saloon. I went on deck at dawn, and could barely stand up against the wind. No land was visible on either side, but, although still very dark, I could just discern the shadowy outline of the iron barge, hovering, like some marine monster, perilously near us, and rising and falling on the crests of the great foaming rollers like an ocean liner in mid-Atlantic. I did not care to think of what would happen if *she* dragged her anchor. The captain, in dripping oilskins and sou'-wester, was pacing the bridge, which he had never left all night, for the engines had been going at half-speed ever since we anchored. The wind was cold and cut through my fur jacket like a knife, so I crawled back to my wet, comfortless cabin, and presently managed to get some sleep, for at six a.m. the wind had dropped, and two hours later the waves had calmed down as rapidly as they had arisen.

The scenery of the Lower Amour is, after leaving Khabarovsk, inexpressibly dreary and monotonous, its low, marshy banks being for miles unrelieved by hill or tree, or indeed by objects of any kind with the exception of the summer *Yourts* of the Gilyaks, and even these are few and far between. An endless succession of sandy promontories, covered with withered herbage and mournful-looking willows, describes the general aspect of the country until we neared Nikolaefsk, when the scenery somewhat improved. There are fifty-two stations between the latter town and Khabarovsk, but we stopped only at a dozen at the most. The majority are tumble-down, squalid-looking settlements, but were interesting on account of the inhabitants,—the queer-looking Gilyaks who inhabit the country between Tambofsk (300 miles south of Nikolaefsk) to the mouth of the Amour, and also, as I have said, parts of the Island of Sakhalin. Here, as on the island, the Gilyaks subsist almost entirely by hunting and fishing, and many of their implements were beautifully wrought and carved. On the second day we reached Nijni-Tambofsk, a desolate-looking village of about 100 houses, clustering round a tiny wooden church, painted a bright pink colour, with a green roof. A curious craft was moored to the bank alongside of us. It looked like a wash-house on the Seine near Paris, but was, I was told, a "Store-barge."

These are fitted out in the spring at Stretynsk with goods of all kinds, and, as soon as the navigation is open, drift slowly down the river, trading with the natives until they reach

GILYAKS, SAKHALIN.

Nikolaefsk, where the barge arrives empty and is broken up. The Gilyaks were swarming round this aquatic emporium like flies round a jam-pot, and the proprietor appeared to be doing a roaring trade. Gold is worked, but only in very small quantities, near Tambofsk.

We reached Sofisk, a still more dreary-looking place than its predecessor, at daybreak on the third day, and at midday Marinsk, which was founded in 1853 by the Russo-American Company, and is, next to Nikolaefsk, the most important settlement on the Lower Amour. But the diversion of trade, caused by the rapidly increasing importance of Vladivostok, has practically ruined all these towns, and Marinsk is little better than the others north of Khabarovsk, either in prosperity or appearance. A collection of dilapidated log huts, perhaps one, or at most two, decent houses belonging to officials, a handful of filthy-looking skin-clad natives, and some mangy dogs and attenuated pigs wallowing in the mire, was the usual *coup d'œil* on arrival at a station on the Lower Amour. An exception was Michaelovsky, a pretty village, surrounded by rich tracts of cultivated land and well-wooded hills, for we had reached a region of trees after a dreary spell of marsh and mud-bank. Rye and barley are grown in considerable quantities around here, and find a ready sale at Nikolaefsk. We approached the village towards sunset, after a glorious day, and as we did so, witnessed a curious sight. Millions of large white moths suddenly surrounded the steamer, and the river, previously glassy as a mirror, became alive with splashing, leaping fish, attracted to the surface by the fluttering insects. The swarm was so dense that, viewed against a background of dark pine forest, it looked like a heavy snowstorm.

At 8 a.m. on the fourth day, we reached Nikolaefsk. No less than three sea-going steamers were lying off the town, a sight that caused all my difficulties to vanish like steam in a tempest, but only, alas! for a time. Experience should have taught me that it is generally easier to enter than to leave Siberia (especially by sea), and, indeed, I shortly discovered that, so far as my needs were concerned, the vessels might as well have been lying at Blackwall. The *Smit*, a Dutch steamer, laden with iron barges for the Amour

Company, was a fixture here for at least six weeks, while the *Hainan* and *Strelok* were both chartered by a Vladivostok firm for trading purposes between Nikolaefsk and Sakhalin, during the open season. I was evidently fated to remain here for an indefinite period, perhaps till the closing of the navigation, when the Russian steamers would be clearing out for Vladivostok.

The dilemma in which I now found myself was considerably increased by the fact that not a lodging of any kind was procurable in the place. Even the proprietor of the small *Traktir*, or brandy shop, declined to receive me as a guest, on the score of want of space, and I returned to the steamer, after a fruitless search, in a very perplexed state of mind. The *Baron Korff* would be returning to Khabarovsk, leaving me high and dry on the little landing-stage, without shelter of any kind. The outlook was anything but cheerful, and I lay down that night hardly comforted by the reflection that my next resting-place would be "à la belle étoile."

The *Baron Korff* was getting up steam the next morning, and I was finally determining, as a forlorn hope, to board one of the steamers in quest of accommodation, when a note was put into my hand. It was sent by Mr. S——, the gentleman whose acquaintance I had made at the Vladivostok railway station, and who had advised me to abandon the land journey to Boussè. Mr. S—— had only just heard of my trouble, and now invited me to be his guest until an opportunity should arise of my leaving Nikolaefsk for the south. Overjoyed at the good news I took leave of the captain, and midday found me watching the departure of the *Baron Korff* from the window of a snug library, well stocked with English books, newspapers, and magazines, and quite resigned to a lengthened stay in such pleasant quarters. Mr. S—— was the manager of the house of Emery & Co, American merchants, well known throughout Eastern Siberia, where they have established a large wholesale and retail business in stores of all kinds in the larger towns. The house (the largest in the place) was sumptuously furnished—a good piano and well-stocked library were luxuries seldom met with in these parts—and had it not been for the ever-present apprehension of being snowed up here for a whole winter, I should have thoroughly enjoyed a visit that I now look back upon as the pleasantest, although perhaps not the most interesting, portion of my journey.

Nikolaefsk, which contains about 3,000 inhabitants, stands on the left bank of the Amour, which is here from three to four miles broad. Sea-going vessels are compelled to anchor in mid-stream, and, during stormy weather, a landing is only effected with great difficulty. Nikolaefsk is now almost in ruins, although the regularity with which the streets are laid out, and the gardens surrounding the tumble-down dwellings, show that it must once have been a pretty and well-kept town, while its situation, on a steep headland overlooking the river for several miles, is highly picturesque. With the exception, however, of Mr. Emery's house, there were not fifty respectable dwellings in the place. All is suggestive of ruin and decay. Empty houses, in every stage of dilapidation, are seen on every side, and even the principal street is a mournful panorama of bulging walls, unhinged gates, and broken railings, fronted by a wilderness of weeds and rank grass where carefully tended shrubs and flowers once gladdened the eye. This dismal thoroughfare terminates abruptly with the prison, a rickety wooden structure, rotting with age and by no means weatherproof. It is now seldom used, save for local offenders. I found only nine inmates, undergoing terms of imprisonment varying from three days to one month. Nikolaefsk once possessed a Government dockyard, but this is now closed, although roofless workshops standing in the midst of neglected machinery, old anchors, and piles of rusty cannon and shot are there to show the strategical as well as commercial downfall of the town, which is now garrisoned by 500 Cossacks and a battery of artillery. The church, with its bright green roof and golden crosses, and Mr. Emery's pretty house with its shady verandahs and gay flower-garden, form the one bright spot in this dreary settlement, which, however, is in summer blessed with a delicious climate and bathed in perpetual sunshine. Nikolaefsk is perhaps the healthiest town in Eastern Siberia. When, in 1894, cholera was raging at Vladivostok and other settlements a few hundred miles south, not a single case occurred here, although there is no water supply except that obtained from the river.

The first week of my stay was thoroughly enjoyable. There was no lack of occupation. My mornings were devoted to literary work, the afternoons to a pleasant stroll in the woods or along the broad sandy beach with a gun (for there is plenty of game and wild fowl), while cards and music enlivened the evenings until bed-time. I usually rose about six a.m. and strolled down to the river-side, where the Gilyaks had established a small fish market. The prices are certainly not ruinous. It would have opened the eyes of Mr. Grove of Bond Street to see salmon of twenty pounds

MAIN STREET OF NIKOLAEFSK.

weight selling at twopence halfpenny apiece, and other fish of various kinds at one shilling per hundred. The latter is salted and used for dog food in the sleighing season. The salmon I found coarse and flavourless when eaten fresh, but, when pickled, palatable enough.

So the days crawled slowly away. A week, ten days, a fortnight elapsed, but still no signs of a vessel of any kind, and this life of enforced inactivity was becoming very irksome. S—— informed me that a small steamer belonging to a Vladivostok firm was advertised to touch here once a month for passengers and cargo. She was now about due, but (like everything else in these latitudes) her dates and movements were very uncertain. I fell into a habit, after a time, of passing my afternoons on the beach gazing out disconsolately, like a male Sister Anne, for the ship that never came.

> Day by day on wall and bastion
> Beat the hollow empty breeze,
> Day by day the sunlight glittered
> On the vacant smiling seas,

but the horizon remained unbroken save for some Gilyak fishing-boat, or a piece of drift-wood, and I generally returned to supper with a resigned conviction that the following spring would find me still here. On the twentieth day, towards evening, a tiny white speck appeared at the mouth of the river, and for a time raised my hopes sky-high, only to dash them to the ground a couple of hours later. The stranger was the *W. J. Colman*, a small schooner eighty days out from San Francisco, and bound for Nikolaefsk with goods for Emery & Co. She was to return to the Golden Gate viâ Kamchatka in a month or so, and was therefore of no avail for my purpose. Strolling home after this disappointment a crowd gathered near the church attracted my attention, and I found on inquiry that a gold miner from the Upper Amour had just been stabbed by an ex-convict from Sakhalin. The latter was at once secured and marched off to prison, where he was eventually flogged and sent back to the island for three years, for his victim died in less than an hour. An attempt was made to lynch him on the way to the jail, but the crowd was driven back at the point of the bayonet by a strong guard of Cossacks summoned from the barracks hard by. S—— told me that such occurrences are frequent here, for quite a third of the population are discharged prisoners. Only three days after this, another murder was committed in our vicinity, a man and his wife being strangled in bed, side by side, while the house was rifled of money and valuables. The perpetrators of the crime escaped, and when I left Nikolaefsk had not been captured. It is thought that they also were expired convicts from Sakhalin.*

Meanwhile, nearly a month had passed away. I had now grown quite resigned to my fate, and discontinuing my visits to the beach, had begun to think seriously about winter clothing. It frequently happens in this world that our wishes are gratified when we least expect it, and so it was with me. Smoking one hot sultry noontide, after breakfast, in the verandah, I lay on a long chair and watched, for some time, a tiny black cloud hovering over the mouth of the river, lazily wondering the while

---

* One of these, an old man over eighty, now living in liberty at Nikolaefsk, has committed *no less than nine murders!*

(for I was half dozing) why, on this glorious day, it was not white. Suddenly a thought roused me like an electric shock, and I leapt from my chair at a bound, bringing S——, who had fallen asleep, to his feet with a startled oath. Then we got glasses, and, after a long inspection, prepared to go down to the beach, for a steamer of some kind or another had arrived at last.

The *Kai-phong* was from Shanghai with a mixed cargo, and was bound for the same port (viâ Japan) "with quick despatch." She was a fine vessel of over 1,200 tons, and having been originally built for the passenger trade, was fitted out with comforts and appliances only to be met with in the luxurious steamships of the far East. Captain Inman, her genial commander, was not impressed with the delights of Siberia, and announced his intention of clearing out, if possible, in four days' time. So, reluctant to trespass further upon my kind host's good-nature and hospitality, I took up my quarters on board without delay. It was a very old and a very dirty boat, but I don't think I have ever felt so overjoyed as I did at finding myself once more under the dear old "Union Jack."

Five days later we were steaming slowly down the Amour, and the *Kai-phong*, being light, had no difficulty in crossing the bar, which is a dangerous one and sometimes detains ships for several days. But, by dusk, we were safely out at sea, and, as the long low land melted away into the mists of evening, I bade farewell, for the third time in my life, to Siberia.

APPENDICES.

Appendix A.
1. Dimensions and tonnage, S.S. *Yaroslav*.
2. Plan of "Kameras," S.S. *Yaroslav*.
3. Diet Scale, S.S. *Yaroslav*.

Appendix B.
1. Plan of Prison at Alexandrovsky-Post.
2. List of clothing supplied to every convict on landing.

Appendix C.
Correspondence on the Onor catastrophe.

Appendix D.
Play-bill of theatrical performance: Sakhalin.

Appendix E.
The escaped Sakhalin Convicts.

Appendix F.
Table of distances and fares: Vladivostok—Nikolaefsk.

Appendix G.
Statistics of death-rate. Mines of Nertchinsk.

Appendix H.
Length of time for wearing fetters.

APPENDIX A.

Dimensions and Tonnage of S.S. *Yaroslav*.

Built at Dumbarton, N.B., by Messrs. Denny & Co., in 1892. A Twin Screw (steel) Steamer.

    Tonnage . . . 3,323 register.
    Length . . . . 409 feet, beam 45 feet.
    Draught . . . 24 feet.
    Ind. Horse-power . . 2,000.

Has nine life-boats (one a steam launch).
Has two condensers to make 5,920 litres a day.
Has seven tanks to contain 15,000 gallons fresh water.
Is lit throughout by electricity and warmed by hot-water pipes.

Has accommodation for 800 convicts, thirty crew, forty engineers and firemen, nine petty officers, and a guard of seventy-two men.

Also for Commander, seven commissioned officers, chaplain, surgeon, and six spare cabins.

Diet Scale on S.S. *Yaroslav*.

Dinner, 11 a.m.; Supper, 5 p.m.

Monday . Dinner: Macaroni Soup (of meat).
          Supper: Gruel and black bread.
Tuesday . Dinner: Cabbage Soup.
          Supper: Rice "Kasha," with butter.

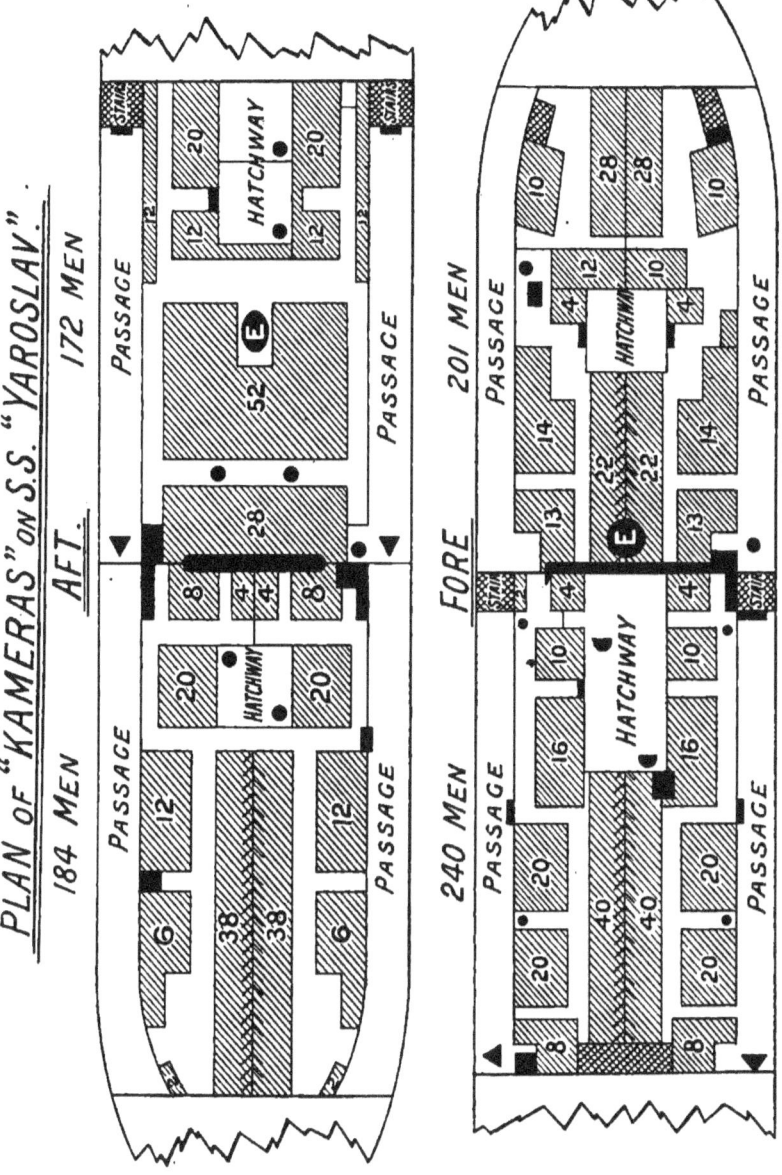

Wednesday . Dinner: Pea Soup and black bread.
　　　　　　Supper: Gruel and black bread.
Thursday . Dinner: Cabbage Soup (with meat).
　　　　　　Supper: Gruel.
Friday .   . Dinner: Cabbage Soup (with oil).
　　　　　　Supper: "Kasha."
Saturday . Dinner: Vermicelli Soup (with meat).
　　　　　　Supper: "Kasha."
Sunday .   . Dinner: Cabbage Soup.
　　　　　　Supper: Gruel and black bread.

Tea (*ad lib.*) at 7 a.m. and 2 p.m.
"Kasha" is a kind of gruel mixed with herbs.

APPENDIX B.

List of Clothing supplied to every Convict on landing on Sakhalin.

3 pairs Canvas Trousers.
3 Canvas "Jumpers."
1 Gray frieze "Khalat" (Overcoat).
1 "Shuba" (Sheepskin Pelisse).
3 Flannel Shirts.
2 Cloth Caps.
2 pairs High Boots, one pair Low Shoes.
6 pairs Flannel Socks.
3 pairs thick Woollen Mitts.

These are to last a year.

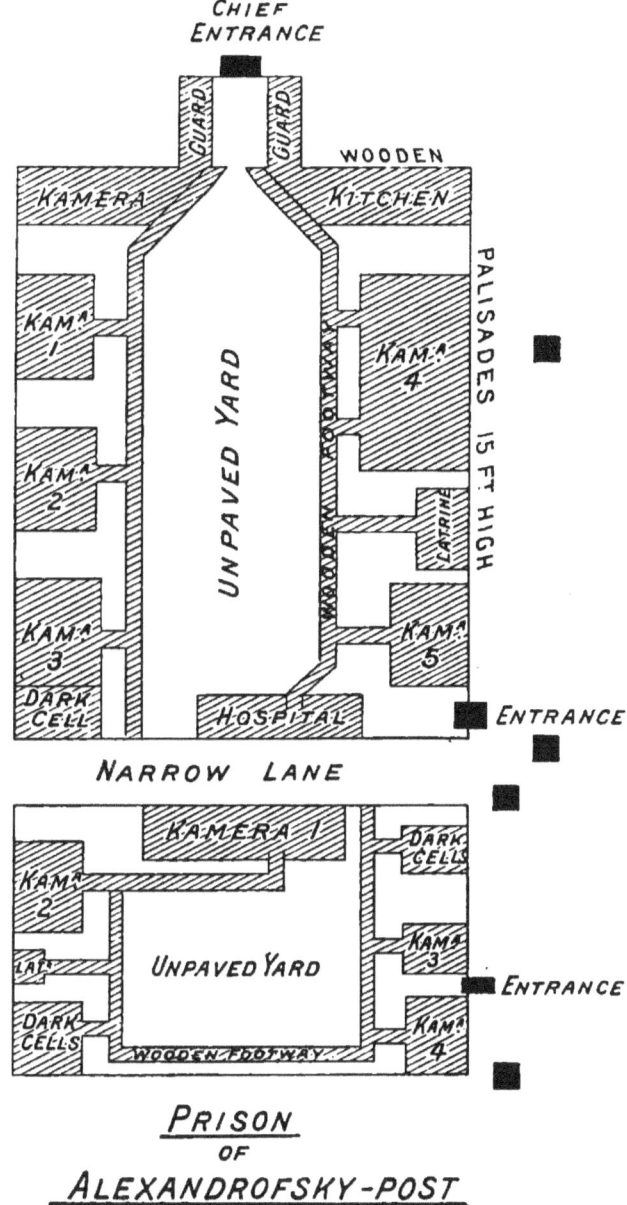

APPENDIX C.

CORRESPONDENCE ON THE ONOR CATASTROPHE.

'THE PRISON OF ONOR.

"*To the Editor of* THE STANDARD.

"SIR,—The following article appears in *The Standard* of February 10th, 1894, as from your St. Petersburg Correspondent:

"'Rumours of the unsatisfactory state of the prison of Onor, in the island of Sakhalin, having reached St. Petersburg, a Government inquiry was instituted some time ago to inquire into the matter. The Report is now to hand, and reveals a terrible tale of suffering and crime. Instances without number are recorded of merciless beatings and lopping-off of fingers and arms by sabre cuts, whilst cannibalism under stress of famine was a common occurrence; murder, followed by cannibalism, being also frequently committed with the sole object of putting an end to the misery of existence at Onor. During the whole of 1892 there was an almost continuous string of convoys with corpses of convicts passing from Onor to Rykovskaya, the residence of the authorities, and the bodies were so mutilated, and presented so pitiful a spectacle, that the spectators could not look upon them without tears. . . . . In 1893, a band of convicts was handed over to an inspector to construct a road from Onor to Rykovskaya. If any convict failed in his work, he was at once put on half rations, the next day followed by one-third of rations, and, when he could work no more, the inspector finished him with a revolver bullet, and entered his death as from disease. The author of these atrocities is the convict Rhakoff, who has been made

Inspector General. The above details are not, it must be noted, a convict's tale, but are taken from an official Government Report. Mr. H. de Windt will probably visit this prison,' amongst others, and it will be curious to see what impression it makes upon him.'

"The above having been widely copied into both English and Continental newspapers, and the writer having seen fit to introduce my name, will you kindly grant me space for a reply, which, as I am writing from the scene of the alleged atrocities, and have questioned, not only the gaoler Khanoff (not Rhakoff), but also the convicts who worked under him at Onor, may throw some light upon the matter. The statement by your Correspondent that the road was being made from Onor to Rykovskaya, instead of *vice versâ*, is, I presume, a misprint. I merely mention this, as even such minor inaccuracies are apt to mislead.

"The facts are these: It was decided in 1892 to build a new prison at Onor, a small Gilyak settlement, about fifty miles south of Rykovskaya. A party of two hundred convicts was accordingly told off (under Khanoff) to make a road (most of it through swamp and *taïga*, or thick jungle) from here to the place in question. The difficulties were numberless; one being the question of supplies, the heavy rains often rendering provisions from Rykovskaya sodden and uneatable. As the party advanced further into the dense forests of the interior, communication became even more difficult, so much so that, upon one occasion, when food at length reached them, both guards and convicts were on the verge of starvation. Thus things went on from bad to worse, until, towards the end of the summer of 1893, they reached a climax, and three of the prisoners resolved to escape. The result was that, after wandering helplessly about the *taïga* for four days, one was murdered while asleep, and partly eaten by his companions, who were shortly afterwards recaptured in a dying condition. Both these men (Vassiliéff and Kalenik) were brought here, tried, and sentenced to ninety lashes with the *plet*, a terrible instrument, now abolished in other parts of Siberia, and only used here in cases of murder. Vassiliéff (whom I saw yesterday) was found to be insane, and was, therefore, spared, but Kalenik was flogged, and died a few days afterwards, of blood-poisoning arising from the punishment. This is the sole case of cannibalism that has occurred at Onor. It can, therefore, scarcely be called 'a common occurrence.'

"I have inquired of many in this village (political exiles amongst them) whether they have ever seen the 'convoys of corpses' described by your Correspondent, but cannot find the slightest ground for such a report. Official statistics return the deaths at Onor (during the eight summer months, extending over two years that the work lasted) as forty-seven, chiefly from fever and dysentery. I was told (and it seems only reasonable) that the difficulty of transport was far too great to admit of bodies being brought back, under any circumstances, for interment at Rykovskaya.

"That mutilation occurred I have had ocular proof in the prison here, but I can safely say that all the wounds I have seen were self-inflicted, for the purpose of shirking work, and being sent back to hospital at Rykovskaya, thus escaping 'the misery of existence at Onor,' which locality, apart from the question of Khanoff's cruelty, must have been, according to all accounts, a perfect hell upon earth for both guards and convicts.

"Khanoff, the gaoler, impressed me most unfavourably. He is hated, not only by the prisoners, but also by the assistant gaolers, one of whom, Mark Niemno, was the means of bringing him to justice. Even Niemno, however, does not accuse Khanoff of ever having wounded, much less slain, any of the Onor gang with a revolver, although there can be no doubt that the man was guilty of the most diabolical cruelty. So far from being made 'Inspector General,' Khanoff is at this moment himself a prisoner here, awaiting the decision of the Commission at St. Petersburg.

"Such is a brief statement of the Onor case, and nothing further will probably transpire until the result of the Government investigation is announced. General Grodékoff, Deputy Governor of Eastern Siberia, is now here collecting evidence, and I have the Governor of Sakhalin's authority for stating that the first official telegram concerning this sad affair was only despatched from here to St. Petersburg towards the end of January, 1893.

"Mr. George Kennan and others have said that Russian prison officials only show me the bright side of things, and that the dark spots of the penal system are cunningly concealed whenever I visit Siberia. If so, is it not strange that upon this occasion the Sakhalin authorities should have gone out of their way to furnish me with the minutest details? Is it not, perhaps, still stranger that they should have volunteered the information that a Siberian convict had died under the lash?

"I am, Sir, your obedient Servant,
"HARRY DE WINDT.

"Rykovskaya, Island of Sakhalin, Sea of Okhotsk,
"*May 28th*, 1894."

APPENDIX D.

PLAY-BILL OF THEATRICAL PERFORMANCE GIVEN BY CONVICTS AT ALEXANDROVSKY-POST,

The original of which is now in the possession of H. BEERBOHM TREE, ESQ.

(PLAY-BILL.)

By permission of His Excellency the Governor, the Amateur Society of Exiles will give a dramatic performance on Friday, the 7th of May, 1894, the proceeds of which will be presented to the "Home for the Children and Orphans of Prisoners" on the Island of Sakhalin.

"THE GOOD ANGEL OF INNOCENCE."

COMEDY IN FOUR ACTS, BY V. KRILOFF.

Characters.

Grigori Yastrebof	SVIETLICHEFF.
Natalia Semenovna	SHOUFSKAYA.
Zina } her Children	{ GRAFOVA.
Boris }	{ MAYEVSKI.
Vassili Moreff	MINAYEFF.
Nadelka (his Daughter)	GIBTCHER.
Jadrinsky	SCHNIDELMANN.
Dousha (Chambermaid)	POMERANTZEFF.
Anton (Laquais)	MITROFANOFF.

"LOOK BEFORE YOU LEAP."

Farce in One Act, by D. Mansfeld.

Alexi Tokni (a Miser) .	Svietlicheff.
Nadia (his Daughter) .	Gibtcher.
Pasha.	Shoufskaya.
Leav Bouroff (a Dandy)	Schnidelmann.
Makarka (his Valet) .	Mitrofanoff.

Performance commences at 8 p.m.

First Seats .	4 Roubles.
Second Seats	2 Roubles.
Third Seats	1 Rouble.
Back Row .	75 Kopeks.

APPENDIX E.

The Escaped Sakhälin Convicts.

Ivan Kovalev, the Russian convict who is to be hanged at Folsom Prison to-morrow for killing aged Mr. and Mrs. Weber, is one of the ten convicts who escaped from the Island of Saghalien in 1893. It is probable that he and his associates were murderers before they got away from the prison island. Two of them had been sentenced by the Russian Government for outrages which merit life imprisonment in this country, but the others claimed when here to have been arrested only for political conspiracy, and there was no contrary evidence. They were all regarded as dangerous criminals when they were under arrest here, and upon releasing the prisoners Captain Lees considered it his duty to deliver, by the aid of an interpreter, a warning lecture on the advisability of obeying the laws of this country.

How much that lecture was needed, and how little attention was paid to it, are shown by this record of three of the men :

One shot dead in San Jose while attempting to rob a store, another sentenced to San Quentin for burglary in San Francisco, and Kovalev to be hanged to-morrow.

Kovalev was regarded by the local officials as the least vicious and dangerous of the lot.

The ten prisoners of the Czar were serving indefinite sentences, according to their testimony, when they found the opportunity to escape from Saghalien. Their story, as told to Walter P. Stradley, the Commissioner of Immigration, was that a Hebrew pedlar rowed to the island in August, 1893, and that, being willing to sell anything that he possessed, he sold his boat to them.

There is an idea, however, that the pedlar was murdered by the convicts in order to obtain the boat, and to prevent the owner from giving information to the authorities.

At any rate, the boat was obtained, and with but little food or water, the convicts started for Japan. They were picked up by an American whaler ten days later, and were brought to this City. Commissioner Stradley arrested them, but after an investigation, the authorities at Washington ordered that the prisoners be released.

The affidavit of Kovalev, signed on November 13th, 1893, is as follows :

"I am twenty-five years of age. I was born in Russia, in the city of Harcov. I am a shoemaker. I know nobody in America. I have no money. In the year 1888 the Russian Government arrested about fifteen Nihilist working men in my native city. I attempted to take their part and help them, and was arrested as a Nihilist.

"I was tried and sent to the island of Saghalien to serve an indefinite sentence. I escaped the same time and in the same manner as my nine companions. I was transferred from the whaler *Charles W. Morgan* to the whaler *Cape Horn Pigeon*, and arrived here on the night of November 9th, 1893.

"IVAN KOVALEV."

The story of the rescue of the ten men is related in the affidavit of Captain J. A. M. Earle, of the American whaling bark *Charles W. Morgan*, as follows :

"On September 3rd, 1893, while in the Okhotsk Sea, about forty miles from the land, and while the boats were down whaling, an open boat came alongside of the bark containing ten Russian subjects, who reported being out ten days in their boat, during three of which they had been without food or water.

"They said that they had escaped from a Siberian prison, and asked to be taken on board. As an act of humanity I complied with their request, for to have left them in that condition would have meant death, especially as a gale came up the next day which would have destroyed their boat.

"I retained them all on board until September 25th, then transferred five of them to the American whaling bark *Cape Horn Pigeon*, for lack of accommodations on my own vessel. The remaining five I gave passage to this port and provided clothing, as they were in a destitute condition when they came on board my ship."

The *Morgan* arrived here on November 7th, 1893, and the *Cape Horn Pigeon* reached port two days later. Kovalev came on the latter vessel. On the arrival of the convicts Commissioner Stradley was notified. Being in doubt whether the immigration laws applied to the case, the latter official telegraphed to Washington for instructions, and he was ordered to arrest and detain the ten men pending an examination. On November 9th the convicts were arrested, the five who arrived on the *Morgan* being then on exhibition at a low-grade saloon theatre on Market Street.

After the testimony had been submitted by Commissioner Stradley, the authorities at Washington decided to release the prisoners. No notification of the reason for the decision accompanied the order of release, but the Commissioner believes that the prisoners were not regarded as immigrants, having been picked up in distress in the open sea and brought here against their will by American vessels.

No interest in the case was ever officially manifested by the Russian Government.

At the release of the prisoners Captain Lees addressed the ten men. He told them that they had come to a free country, where they could enjoy all the advantages afforded to any others. They would have a good deal of liberty here, he said, but the people in this country would not tolerate the manifestation of any nihilistic or anarchistic tendencies. If any of them should become lawless they would have to accept the punishment.

That ended the warning. To-morrow the threatened punishment will be meted out to a third member of the gang.

(From *San Francisco Examiner*, March 5th, 1896.)

APPENDIX F.

TABLE OF DISTANCES AND FARES FROM VLADIVOSTOK TO NIKOLAEFSK.

	Versts.	Roubles.
Vladivostok—Boussè	352	5
Boussè—Khabarovsk	454	12
Khabarovsk—Stretynsk	2,017	50
Stretynsk — Alexandrovsky - Zavod, Akatui, and back to Stretynsk	557	30
Stretynsk—Khabarovsk	2,017	50
Khabarovsk—Nikolaefsk	940	23
Total { Versts	6,337	170 Roubles
or English miles	4,210	or £17

APPENDIX G.

STATISTICS OF DEATH-RATE. MINES OF NERTCHINSK.

MONSIEUR,—Conformément aux instructions du Général Gouverneur et en réponse à vos questions, je m'empresse de vous communiquer les détails suivants sur les travaux forcés de Nertchinsk.

1. Nombre des décès parmi les forçats aux mines de Nertchinsk :

En 1891 hommes 79, femmes 15.
„ 1892   „   66,   „   7.
„ 1893   „   51,   „   11.

2. Nombre des accidents :

Le 26 mars, 1893, le forçat Chamanoff, détenu dans la prison d'Algatchi, tomba d'une échelle dans le puits de mine et mourut des suites des lésions reçues pendant la chute.

3. Le 12 janvier, 1894, six forçats étant descendus dans le puits de la mine de Vozdaïansky et s'étant mis à forer, l'explosion subite d'une cartouche de dynamite blessa grièvement deux des forçats, dont l'un mourut le lendemain.

3. Les maladies les plus fréquentes parmi les forçats de Nertchinsk pendant les années 1891, 1892, et 1893, ont été : fièvre intermittente, péripneumonie chronique, catarrhe d'estomac et des intestins, syphillis, inflammation tuberculeuse des poumons, maladies cutanées, fractures, déboîtements, blessures, maladies vénériennes, scorbut, ophtalmie, dérangements psychiques.

4. Les rapports de l'administration des mines de Nertchinsk pour les années 1891, 1892 et 1893 ne mentionnent aucune épidémie.

5. Nombre des forçats évadés des mines de Nertchinsk :

En 1891 hommes 81, femmes 3.
,, 1892 ,, 70, ,, 3.
,, 1893 ,, 85, ,, 5.

6. A défaut d'un médecin spécial attaché au service médical des forçats de Nertchinsk, ces derniers sont à la charge de médecins appartenant à d'autres administrations et qui reçoivent à cet effet un salaire additionnel. Ainsi l'hôpital de Kara, qui, autrefois, comptait jusqu'à 250 lits, était desservi par le médecin du second bataillon d'infanterie des Cosaques. Dans les arrondissements d'Algatchi, de Zérentouï, et dans la prison d'Acatouï, jusque vers le milieu de l'année 1891, le service médical incombait au médecin divisionnaire de la 3e section militaire. Puis, jusqu'en février, 1893, à un médecin de l'administration des mines, et enfin,

dès cette date, un médecin praticien libre fut invité à remplir ces fonctions.

Les mines de Nertchinsk comptent quatre hôpitaux, à chacun desquels est attaché un officier de santé exerçant ses fonctions sous la direction du médecin principal des mines.

Veuillez agréer, Monsieur, l'assurance de ma parfaite considération.

Le Vice-Gouverneur de la Circonscription
du Trans-Baïkal, Conseiller d'Etat,
N. NITZKEVITSKY.

TCHITA, *ce 29 Septembre-Octobre*, 1894.

APPENDIX H.

LENGTH OF TIME FOR WEARING FETTERS.

A convict sentenced:

For life	8 years	in chains.
,, 20 years	4 ,,	,,
,, 12 ,,	2 ,,	,,
,, 6 ,,	1½ ,,	,,
,, 4 ,,	1 ,,	,,
,, 2 ,,	6 months	,,
,, 1, ,,	3 ,,	,,

INDEX.

AIGUN, the city of, 221, 222
Ainus, the, 113
Akatui, 236; political prison at, 255-263; climate of, 272
Albazin, the town of, 231
Alexandrovsky-Post, 81, 86; landing of prisoners at, 82; prisons at, 81, 90; freed workmen at, 100; schools and orphanage at, 106; playbill of theatrical performance given by convicts at, 312
Alexandrovsky-Zavod, 254
Amour, the Upper, 188, 195, 212; Steam Navigation Company, 195; navigation on the, 204, 212; journey on the, 209
Amour, the Lower, 283-288; storm on the, 286
Archangelski, Colonel, Governor of the prison at Akatui, 258
Arkovo, the village of, 118

BAIKAL, Lake, 148, 239
Baron Korff, the, 209, 211; luncheon party on board the, 210; travelling companions on the, 212; collision with another steamer, 219
Blagovieshtchensk, the town of, 223, 225
Bloeffstein, Sophie (the Golden Hand), 129-135
Boussè, the village of, 142, 188; post house at, 189-194

Boutakoff, Mons., the Commandant of Rykovskaya, 120, 130, 136
Bureya, the river, 216

CEREALS, trade in, done by the Chinese, 215
Collision on the river Amour, 217-221
Convicts, on the *Yaroslav*, 2; evening service of, 7; number of, on board, 15; clothing of, 18, 306; food of, 19, 63, 264, 305; description of, 24; cruelty of, to each other, 25; criminal, at Sakhalin, 53; freed, 55; punishments of, 58, 60; classes of criminal, 58; employments of freed, 59, 69, 104; privileges of freed, 60; at Korsakovsky prison, 53-59; story of ten, at Mauka, 76; landing of, at Alexandrovsky-Post, 82-86; pardon of a, 84; appearance of, at Alexandrovsky-Post, 97; an ex-convict, Mons. L., 234; journey of, to silver mines, 237-240; at Gorni-Zerentui, 249; wives and families of, 250-252; at Akatui, 264; escaped Siberian, 313
Cossacks, 189, 197; of the Oussouri, 190, 229

DENBIGH'S, MR., account of Sakhalin, 72-79

Y

Derbynskaya, village of, 120; prison at, 122, 135
Dobrovoilno Flott (Volunteer Fleet), 9
Dogs, sledges with, 51; sleigh, 69, 113
Dui, village of, 58, 90

EMIGRANTS, free, 237
Étapes, 238, 239
Exiles to Siberia, 237; journey to the mines of, 238, 239; wives of political, 252; political, 257, 264-282; grades of political exile, 263; books read by political, 269, 276

FELLOW-COUNTRYMEN, meeting with, 72, 145; hospitality of, 293
Fellow-travellers, 143-165; 174-177; 179; 189; 192, 194, 196; 212
Floods, 143, 159-164

GILYAK village and people, 112-117, 288
Girin, city of, 215
Gold mines, 223, 257, 289
Goldi, the, people, 197
Gorni-Zerentui, village of, 236, 245; prison at, 247-250; orphanage at, 252
Graf Putiyatin, the, 195
Grodekoff, General, 196-201

HOSPITAL at Korsakovsky, 67; Rykovskaya, 128; Akatui, 266, 272

IMPLEMENTS of punishment, 92-94

Insects, 148, 189, 192, 195; preventive against mosquitoes, 183; swarm of white moths, 291
Interviews with political exiles, 266-276
Irkoutsk, 239

JOURNEY in the Interior, 111-137; difficult, from Vladivostok to Nova-Silya, 142-165; from Nova-Silya to Boussè, 167-186; up the Oussouri river, 195-201; up the Amour, 209-232; from Stretynsk to Nertchinsk, 236; of convicts from Europe to the mines of the Trans-Baikal, 237-240; return from Stretynsk to Tchernigovka, 283-302

K., MONS., a Russian engineer, 143-165
Kai-phong, the, 301
Kalenik, the convict, 103, 310
Kameras, of the *Yaroslav*, 3; inspection of, 10; description of, 15-17; at Korsakovsky-Post, 63-66; at Alexandrovsky-Post, 92, 97; at Rykovskaya, 124-127; at Gorni-Zerentui, 248; at Akatui, 263
"Katorga, The ten men of," 77-79
Kazarm, 184
Khabarovsk, 142, 200-207; military force at, 204
Khanoff, a gaoler, 136, 310
Korsakovsky-Post, 52; convicts at, 53, 54; Governor's house at, 55-58; prison of, 61; con-

victs' food at, 62 ; prison workshops at, 66 ; school at, 67 ; infirmary at, 67

Koslovski, village of, 198, 199

LANDING of convicts, 82-86

Lepsky, Mitza, 37
——— Serge, 38 ; arrest of, 44 ; sentence of, 47 ; landing of, 85

MANCHU, the, people, 197

Marinsk, the town of, 290

Mauka, fishing trade at, 73 ; trade in skins at, 74 ; story of ten convicts escaped from, 76-79

Merkazine, General, Governor of the Island of Sakhalin, 81

Michaelovsky, village of, 290

Mines, the silver, of Nertchinsk, 233-282 ; labour in, 265 ; inspection of, 278; statistics of death-rate at, 317

Mines, gold, 223, 257, 289

Mouravieff, General, Governor-General of Khabarovsk, 190, 203 ; dinner with, 207

Mutiny, precautions against, on the *Yaroslav*, 20

NAGASAKI, 1

Nertchinsk, silver mines of, 233-282

Nijni-Tambofsk, village of, 288

Nikolaefsk, 291, 294-296 ; hospitality of Mr. S. at, 293 ; prison at, 295 ; composition of population of, 300

OFFICERS, Russian, pay of, 200

Olga Elnikoff, 5, 22 ; story of, 31-49 ; 85, 109, 110

Onor, the, tragedy, 100, 308

Orphanage at Alexandrovsky-Post, 106 ; at Gorni-Zerentui, 250-253

Oussouri, the river, 183, 188 ; journey up the, 195-201 ; races on either bank, 197

PASHCHENKO, a notorious convict, 100-102

Penal establishments, 122, 247 ; permit to inspect, 208

Plet, the, 60, 93

Pokorovsky, special prison for women, 279

Political exiles — Göttze, 266-271 ; Khotchurikin, 274, 276 ; Minor, 274, 275 ; Ouflandt, 274; Slavinsky, 271, 272, 276 ; Vraginsky, 266-271

Polyakoff, the Russian explorer, 58

Por-na-maré, 68-70

Post houses :—at Polustianok, 173 ; fellow-travellers at, 173-177 ; at Shmakovka, 179 ; at Rijova, 183 ; at Boussè, 186-194 ; at Shalopougina, 241 ; at Staina, 244 ; Siberian post house at night, 241

Prisons : — Korsakovsky-Post, 61-68 ; Alexandrovsky-Post, 81-109 ; Rykovskaya, 122-129 ; Derbynskaya, 122, 135 ; Gorni-Zerentui, 246-254 ; Akatui, 255-282 ; Nikolaefsk, 295

Prison clothing, 15, 124, 266, 306

Punishment, grades of, 59, 68, 98 ; implements of, 92-94 ; cells, 100

Psyche, the, 127, 128

RAILWAY, the Trans-Siberian, 142, 146–150, 178, 179
Regiments, method of moving, in Siberia, 230
Rijova, post house at, 183
Rivers:—the Amour, Upper, 188, 195, 201–232; the Lower, 281–302; the Bureya, 216; the Oussouri, 182, 183, 189–201; the Shilka, 231; the Soungari, 215; the Zeya, 213, 223
Roché, M. de, 224
Rykovskaya, 111, 120; prison at, 122–127; school at, 127; hospital at, 128

SAKHALIN, the island of, 28, 50–53; arrival at, 51; seasons at, 51, 59, 117; criminal convicts at, 58–61; law relating to foreign convicts at, 71; Mr. Denbigh's account of, 72–79; Governor of, 81; freed convicts at, 105; native population of, 113–117
Schools for children of prisoners, 67, 106, 127, 199
Shafts in the silver mines, 278, 279
Shalopougina, post house at, 241
Shilka, the river, 231
Shmakovka, post house at, 179
Siberian exile system, 75, 135, 190
Skins, in the rough, 74
Skobeltzina, 216
Sokoloff, the convict, 105
Soungari, the river, 215
Spask, the town of, 155–157
Squadron, the Russian Pacific, 141

Staina, postmaster at, 244
Starosta, the, cruelty of, 26
Store-barge at Nijni-Tambofsk, a, 288
Stretynsk, 233–236
Switzerland, the Siberian, 243

TARAKANS, 189, 192
Tarantass, breakdown of the, 152, 155
Taskine, Mr., Governor of Alexandrovsky prison, 89
Tchernayeff, 229
Tchernigovka, the village of, 142; at the station of, 151
Telega, country cart or, 169; driver of, 171, 180–184; drive on a, 180, 181
Tomiline, Mons., Governor of the prison at Gorni-Zerentui, 246

VASSILIEF, the convict, 68
Vladivostok, 138–143; railway-station at, 144–146; table of distance and fares from, to Nikolaefsk, 317
Vologdine, Mons., Governor of Korsakovsky prison, 53–58

WHEELBARROWS, convicts chained to, 59, 98
Wives and families of convicts in the penal settlements, 250–254; of political exiles, 252

Yaroslav, the Prison Ship, 1–30; dimensions and tonnage of, 304

ZEYA, the river, 213, 223